VISUAL DICTIONARY

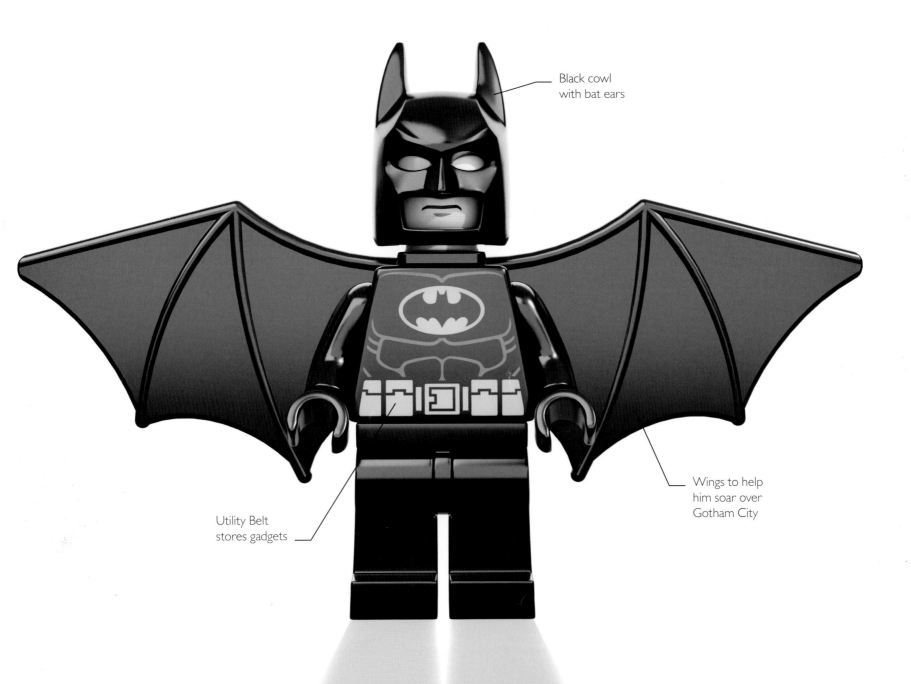

Black cowl
with bat ears

Wings to help
him soar over
Gotham City

Utility Belt
stores gadgets

Fin is shaped
like a bat's wing

Batwoman

Copper
bat-symbol

VISUAL DICTIONARY

Written by

Elizabeth Dowsett and Arie Kaplan

Missile
launchers

Aerodynamic
bat ears

BATJET

CONTENTS

INTRODUCTION

The LEGO® Group has been bringing the DC Comics world into LEGO® form since 2006. In the LEGO DC Super Heroes theme, Batman, Superman, Wonder Woman, and their Justice League friends fight crime and battle the world's worst super-villains using all their amazing LEGO vehicles, weapons, and gadgets.

Jump inside the Batmobile, load up the Flying Fox, grab that stud shooter, board Wonder Woman's Invisible Jet, and enter Arkham Asylum. Build your very own top-secret Batcave, and even build Batman himself! There's never a dull moment with battles to be won and minifigures who need to be rescued.

From movies to Mighty Micros, there are many more exciting things to come for LEGO Batman, his allies, and his foes! Stay tuned!

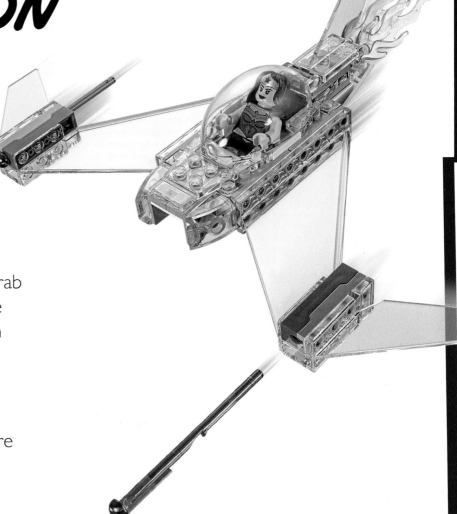

DATA BOXES

Throughout the book, each LEGO DC Super Heroes set is identified with a data file, which provides the official name of the set, the year of its first release, the LEGO identification number, the number of LEGO pieces—or elements—in the set, and the number of minifigures in the set.

Set name	App-Controlled Batmobile	
Year 2018	**Number** 76112
Pieces 321	**Minifigures** 1

TIMELINE

The first ever LEGO® Batman leaped into action fighting crime in 2006. Other Super Heroes joined Batman in 2012 when the LEGO DC Super Heroes theme was born and it expanded to include Mighty Micros, polybags, and LEGO Dimensions packs. After THE LEGO® BATMAN MOVIE was released, collectable minifigures and many more awesome sets were added. Let's look at some of the highlights!

2006

The LEGO Batman theme was launched in 2006

The Batman Dragster: Catwoman Pursuit (7779)
Batman's first LEGO vehicle

The Batcave: The Penguin and Mr. Freeze's Invasion (7783)
The first LEGO Batcave and the first LEGO Batman set of more than 1,000 pieces

2008

LEGO Batman: The Videogame
Fans of LEGO Batman first took to their consoles to join their hero on missions

2012

The Batmobile: Ultimate Collector's Edition (7784)
The first LEGO Ultimate Collector's Edition for the theme

2012

The LEGO DC Super Heroes theme was launched in 2012

The Batcave (6860)
The second LEGO Batcave set is released

Batman Jet Surfer (30160)
Batman fights crime in his first LEGO DC Super Heroes polybag set

Batman (4526)
The first buildable Batman is released

LEGO Batman 2: DC Super Heroes
The second LEGO Batman video game comes to consoles worldwide

---

2013

Batman: Arkham Asylum Breakout (10937)
After first appearing in 2006, a second creepy Arkham Asylum set is released

Superman: Metropolis Showdown (76002)
Superman's first starring role in a LEGO set

2014

The Tumbler (76023)
The second Ultimate Collector's Edition in the theme is released

LEGO Batman 3: Beyond Gotham
The third LEGO Batman video game sees Batman battling in many new environments

LEGO® Dimensions Starter Pack Xbox One (71172)
The first ever LEGO Dimensions starter pack to include Batman

Jokerland (76035)
The first time the Joker gets his own large set

Batman Classic TV Series Batcave (76052)
This set is based on the classic 1960s TV series and has the most pieces in a LEGO DC Super Heroes set ever!

Mighty Micros: Batman vs. Catwoman (76061)
The first LEGO DC Super Heroes Mighty Micros set makes its appearance

Knightcrawler Tunnel Attack (76086)
The Super Heroes team up in the first Justice League LEGO set

Flying Fox: Batmobile Airlift Attack (76087)
This set comes with a Batmobile as well as a huge Flying Fox carrier vehicle

THE LEGO® BATMAN MOVIE
is released into movie theaters worldwide

The Joker Manor (70922)
The Joker creates more mayhem with his renovation of Wayne Manor

Arkham Asylum (70912)
The third LEGO Arkham Asylum set is based on the location from the THE LEGO BATMAN MOVIE

Mighty Micros: Superman vs. Bizarro (76068)
The first time we see Superman in a LEGO DC Super Heroes Mighty Micros set

Batwing Adventure (10823)
Younger fans are introduced to Batman with this set for 2-to-5-year-olds in a LEGO® DUPLO® set

The Bat-Space Shuttle (70923)
Batman and friends journey into outer space in this large set

App-Controlled Batmobile (76112)
An amazing app-controlled Batmobile—the first of its kind in this theme

LEGO DC Super-villains
The fourth LEGO Batman video game is released

CHAPTER 1:
SUPER HEROES

Printed black seams

BATMAN

Meet Batman! He's the world-famous Super Hero who wears a black mask with two pointy bat ears. Also known as the Caped Crusader, he fights crime in Gotham City, chasing criminals and fighting villains. He's a skilled martial artist and has tons of amazing gadgets and equipment stashed in his Utility Belt.

◄ CAPED CRUSADER

This Batman from 2017 drives the huge Knightcrawler tank when he teams up with the Justice League. His unique Batsuit has flecks of silver printing on the torso and legs to look like armor weave.

Five-pointed cape is like the bat-symbol

BATARANG

BATSHIELD

BAT-GEAR

Batman has invented a ton of awesome gadgets and weapons to help him fight crime. His most used is his Batarang, and he has a new Batshield.

THRASHER BATMAN

A heavily armored Batman fights the Talon Assassins wearing a metallic suit, and his helmet has red eyes.

DESERT BATMAN

Batman dons a sandy-colored suit to rescue Robin from Rā's al Ghūl's desert hideout.

SPACE BATMAN

Space Batman has two capes: one with wings out; one with wings folded for flying with a rocket pack.

ARCTIC BATMAN

This is the only all-white Batman. He is ready to face off in the snow against Mr. Freeze.

▼ MIGHTY MICROS BATCOPTER

Batman swaps his signature black vehicles for a bright red one with his Mighty Micros Batcopter. He flies this speedy, compact helicopter in an aerial battle against the villain Killer Moth.

A red LEGO® brick with the bat-symbol

Rotor blades spin

Cloak billows in the wind

Bat-symbol on bright yellow

Simplified Utility Belt

TINY BATMAN

As the second Batman minifigure in a Mighty Micros set, this is the second one to have short legs, but he doesn't look very happy about it. This is the first in blue and gray.

Set name		
Mighty Micros: Batman vs. Killer Moth		
Year 2017		
Number 76069		
Pieces 83		
Minifigures 2		

TACTICAL BATMAN

As a member of the Justice League, Batman's minifigure has a tactical suit with a flight harness. It has reflective silver printing and a gold Utility Belt.

Batman is unshaven

Flight harness

Stud shooters

Set name
Flying Fox: Batmobile Airlift Attack

Year 2017   **Number** 76087

Pieces 955   **Minifigures** 6

▲ JUSTICE LEAGUE BATMOBILE

Race through the streets with this 2017 Batmobile based on the one driven by Batman in the 2017 movie *Justice League*. It has swapped half of its cockpit for a heavy-duty cannon. As well as the highways of Gotham City, it also travels the skies, as it fits into the Flying Fox carrier.

1960S BATMAN

Classic Batman swoops in wearing dark-blue pants over sand-blue tights and dark-blue boots. He also has a dark-blue cowl with printed details.

▼ CLASSIC BATMOBILE

Back in the 1960s, *Batman* was a popular TV series. This LEGO Batmobile is based on the one in the show, which in turn was based on the 1955 Lincoln Futura car. It's design is classic of the era, with a long, thin, rectangular body and long tail fins.

Slicked-down hair

Open-necked shirt with ascot

Red Batphone

Red trim matches the car from the TV series

Set name
Batman Classic TV Series—Batcave

Year 2016   **Number** 76052

Pieces 2526   **Minifigures** 9

Hubcaps printed with bat-symbol

BRUCE WAYNE

Behind the Batsuit is dapper Bruce Wayne. He inherited a fortune from his parents, including the huge company Wayne Industries. He now uses his wealth to invent and build many of Batman's vehicles and weapons.

FLYING FOX

How can the Batmobile fly? In the Flying Fox, of course! This massive vehicle carrier is just one of the latest products from the company Wayne Technology. It's a huge, winged platform with a cockpit on top for transporting Batman's Batmobile around, along with the rest of the Justice League team.

Set name
Flying Fox: Batmobile Airlift Attack

Year 2017　　　**Number** 76087

Pieces 955　　　**Minifigures** 6

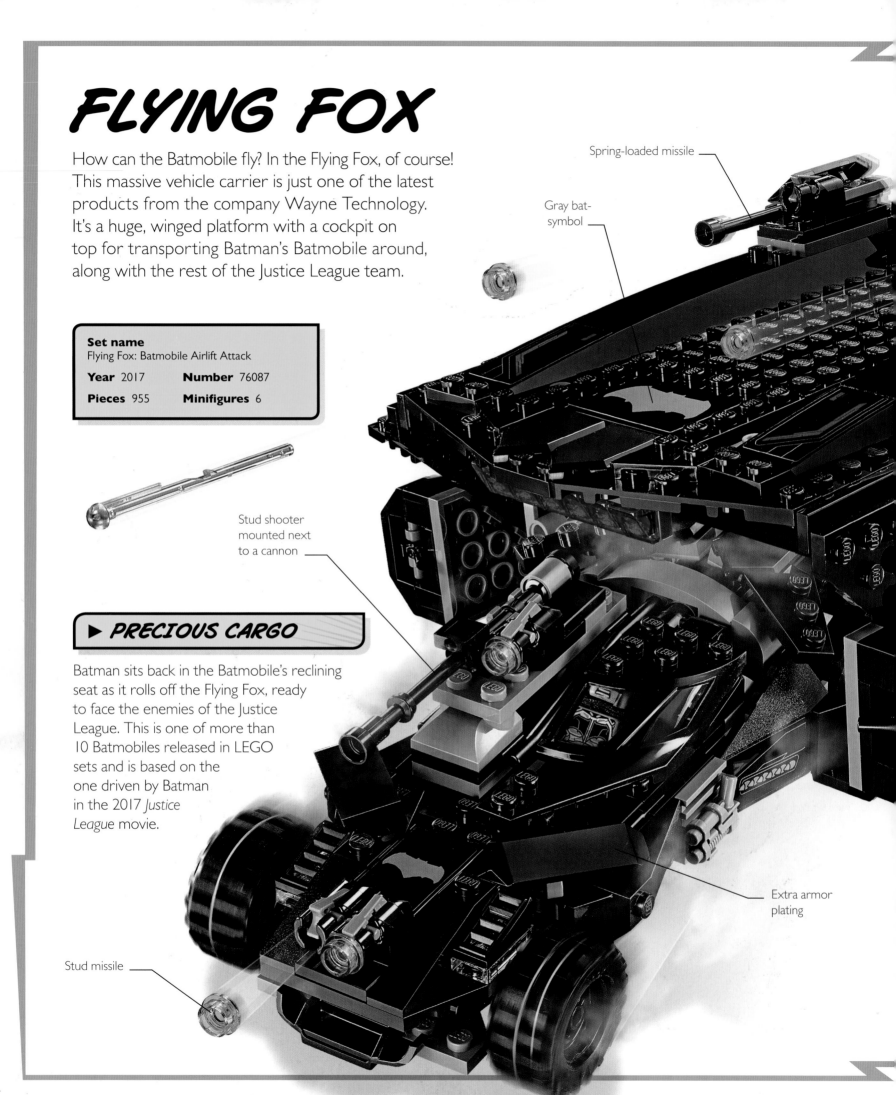

Spring-loaded missile

Gray bat-symbol

Stud shooter mounted next to a cannon

Extra armor plating

Stud missile

▶ PRECIOUS CARGO

Batman sits back in the Batmobile's reclining seat as it rolls off the Flying Fox, ready to face the enemies of the Justice League. This is one of more than 10 Batmobiles released in LEGO sets and is based on the one driven by Batman in the 2017 *Justice League* movie.

Pilot flies from the back of the vehicle

Angled, aerodynamic fins

Wheel piece is one of the two engines

Lattice roof tiles for air vents

Wing hinges

Door hatch is marked "Wayne Technology"

Wing obscures a spring-loaded shooter

Wing tip hinges separately from the main wing

JUSTICE LEAGUE

In this set, an exclusive Batman minifigure teams up with a brand-new Cyborg, Superman, and Wonder Woman to protect the red Mother Box—a powerful supercomputer—from Steppenwolf and his Parademons.

COCKPIT

The cockpit holds two minifigures behind transparent red plastic, which allows a 360-degree view. Two pilots can sit back-to-back, and each has their own console to control the vehicle and its missiles.

▲ LARGE CARRIER AIRCRAFT

Designed by Bruce Wayne as a flying carrier for the Batmobile, the Flying Fox is both armed and armored. Its huge lower deck is completely open so Batman's car can drive on from either the front or the back. Once the car is secured in place with rubber tabs on the ceiling and hinged pieces on the floor, the Flying Fox is cleared for takeoff!

BATMAN IN FLIGHT

Batman has earned his wings with his collection of amazing flying machines. They are perfect for chasing, swooping, dogfighting, and showing off with acrobatics. These incredible Batwings, Batcopters, and Bat-Gliders give the Caped Crusader the wing power he needs to fight crime.

Set name
Heroes of Justice: Sky High Battle

Year 2016   **Number** 76046

Pieces 517   **Minifigures** 5

Vertical stabilizers are poseable

The two cockpit canopy pieces split and open up so they look like two bat ears

► THE BATWING

Soaring over Metropolis, the Batwing rescues Lois Lane from Lex Luthor. This mean-looking machine is in flying mode, but can be instantly switched to takeoff mode by flicking a lever at the back, which makes both wings flip up to be vertical.

Rapid-fire stud shooter

Wings in flight mode

New copper bat-symbol pieces

◄ BATJET

Batman and Batwoman use this jet to take down Brother Eye and the O.M.A.C. (One Man Army Corps) cyborg. The aerodynamic flying machine looks like a bat from the front when it's flying at you and also when seen from above.

Set name
Batman: Brother Eye Takedown

Year 2018   **Number** 76111

Pieces 269   **Minifigures** 3

Front prongs look like bat ears from above

► THE BAT

Swoop to Commissioner Gordon's rescue in the Bat. It's a flying battle machine with a rope for winching up Jim Gordon so he can escape Bane in the Tumbler. The LEGO Bat is full of hinges so can be manipulated to fly in many different ways.

Set name	The Bat vs. Bane: Tumbler Chase	
Year 2013	**Number** 76001	
Pieces 368	**Minifigures** 3	

There's room for Commissioner Gordon in the back seat

Rotor blade piece

Large bat tail fin

The only LEGO Batcopter with a six-bladed rotor

◄ THE BATCOPTER

The black-and-blue Batcopter has a hidden function. When you push the tail boom into the cockpit, panels on the sides pop out and reveal stud shooters. They can be fired by hand, or, if you gently push the panels in, they will fire automatically.

Set name		
Batman: Scarecrow Harvest of Fear		
Year 2016		
Number 76054		
Pieces 563		
Minifigures 5		

Gas mask worn by Batman because of Scarecrow's fear gas

1x1 roof tile creates curved effect

► THE BAT-GLIDER

For true versatility in the air, Batman doesn't want to be weighed down by a whole vehicle. He can react nimbly with the Bat-Glider that is a mechanical pair of wings attached to his torso with a clear bracket.

Set name	Lex Luthor Mech Takedown	
Year 2018	**Number** 76097	
Pieces 406	**Minifigures** 5	

Thrusters

New comic-style power bursts

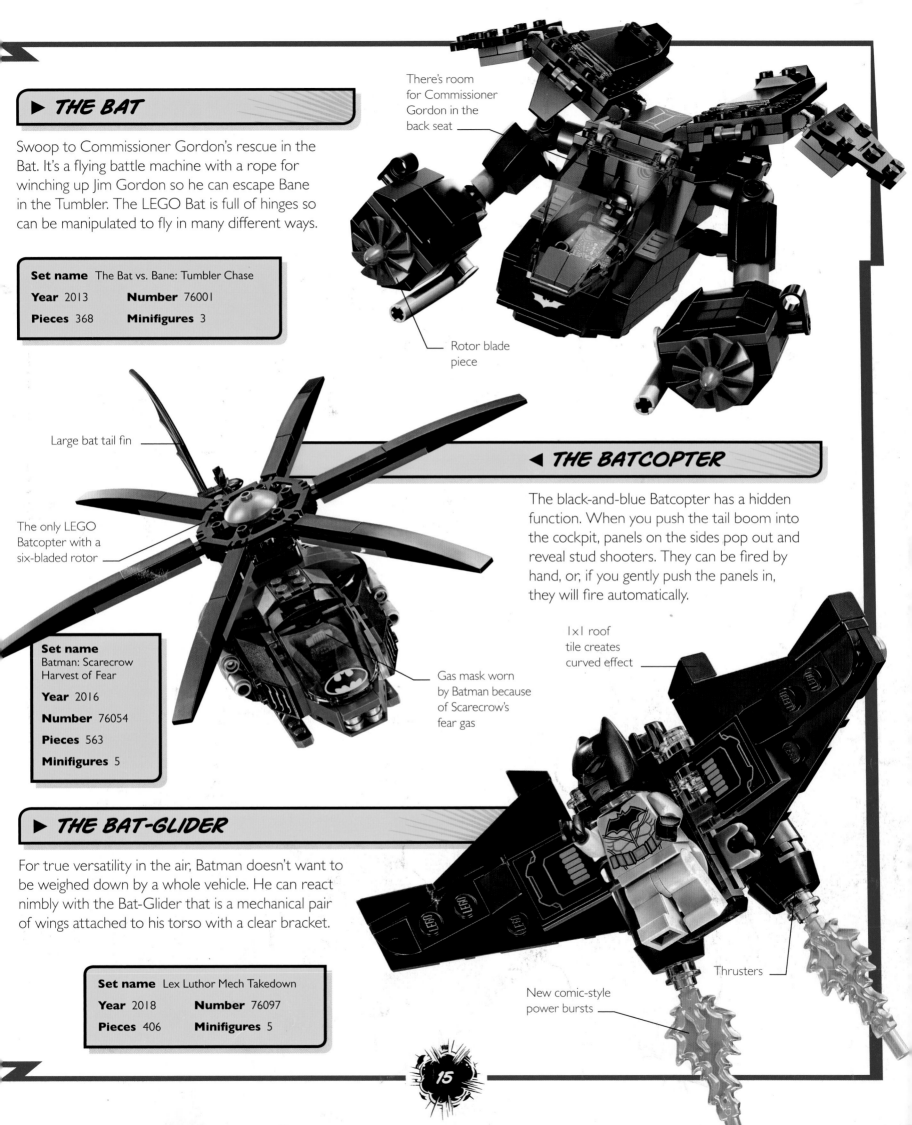

BATMAN'S WHEELS

Villains beware! Batman has cars, tanks, motorbikes, buggies, and mechs. If they try to escape, the Caped Crusader will be after them to deliver swift justice, whether on wheels, treads, or mechanical feet. These vehicles are armored and dangerous. Fighting crime is a serious business!

Low-slung driving seat

Six-stud shooter

Caterpillar tracks

Set name Batman: Killer Croc Sewer Smash

Year 2016

Number 76055

Pieces 759

Minifigures 4

▶ THE BAT-TANK

The sturdy, four-treaded Bat-Tank is just what Batman needs against Killer Croc's Battle Chomper. Turn the engine piece at the back to rotate the front section up and forward. This creates a bat-shaped battering ram for attacking with brute force.

Thrasher Batman

Bat-symbol on wheel hub

◀ BAT-BIKE

With red eyes on the front, this Bat-bike looks as fierce as Batman does in his new Thrasher armor. He is souped-up and ready to challenge the Talon Assassins on this rugged, three-wheeled bike.

New yellow bat piece

Set name	The Attack of the Talons
Year 2018	**Number** 76110
Pieces 155	**Minifigures** 3

Windshield wipers

▶ THE TUMBLER

The Tumbler is heavily armored and has big racing tires and adjustable top wings. The Tumbler is an Ultimate Collector's Set: a large detailed set designed for collectors.

Set name	The Tumbler
Year 2014	**Number** 76023
Pieces 1869	**Minifigures** 2

Tires are nearly twice the height of a minifigure

16

◄ THE BATCYCLE

Lying forward in the seat, Batman rides this hefty Batcycle to battle Harley Quinn and Deadshot. The large, wide wheels keep him stable while he fires the grappling gun, stud shooters, and Batarang.

— Stud shooter

Set name
Batman: Gotham City Cycle Chase

Year 2016

Number 76053

Pieces 224

Minifigures 3

▼ DESERT BATMAN'S BUGGY

Many vehicles would get bogged down in sand, but not Batman's buggy. It's just what he needs for whizzing across the desert to reach Rā's al Ghūl's desert hideout, where Robin is being held. Minifigures climb in and out by lifting the roll bars.

Roll bars

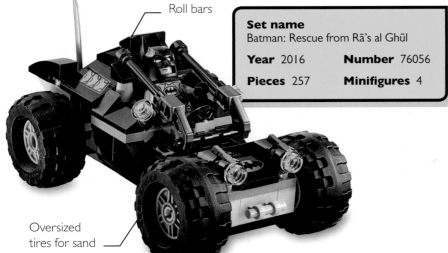

Set name
Batman: Rescue from Rā's al Ghūl

Year 2016   **Number** 76056

Pieces 257   **Minifigures** 4

Oversized tires for sand

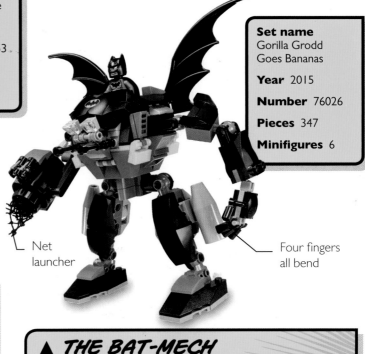

Set name
Gorilla Grodd Goes Bananas

Year 2015

Number 76026

Pieces 347

Minifigures 6

Net launcher

Four fingers all bend

▲ THE BAT-MECH

Batman sits high up to control the weapons in this mech. He can even use the super-jumper function to leap at Grodd the Gorilla's big figure. The mech is very agile and moves smoothly.

► BLUETOOTH BATMOBILE

Batman has a new, compact Batmobile in his Batcave garage. This is the first ever Bluetooth-controlled LEGO Batman vehicle! Using an app to control the armored car remotely, it can move forward, backward, left, and right, and even spin 360 degrees.

Power button

Set name App-Controlled Batmobile

Year 2018   **Number** 76112

Pieces 321   **Minifigures** 1

Heavily armored

O.M.A.C. CRISIS

Batman and Batwoman face a real robot rampage as flying Brother Eye orders his O.M.A.C. cyborg to attack. On the ground, Batman has to dodge the O.M.A.C.'s power blasts and hope he can take down the cyborg with a well-aimed Batarang. Meanwhile, up in the sky, Batwoman maneuvers her Batjet to shoot down Brother Eye. If she can just hit Brother Eye in the eye, she'll be able to put a stop to the rogue satellite's dastardly schemes!

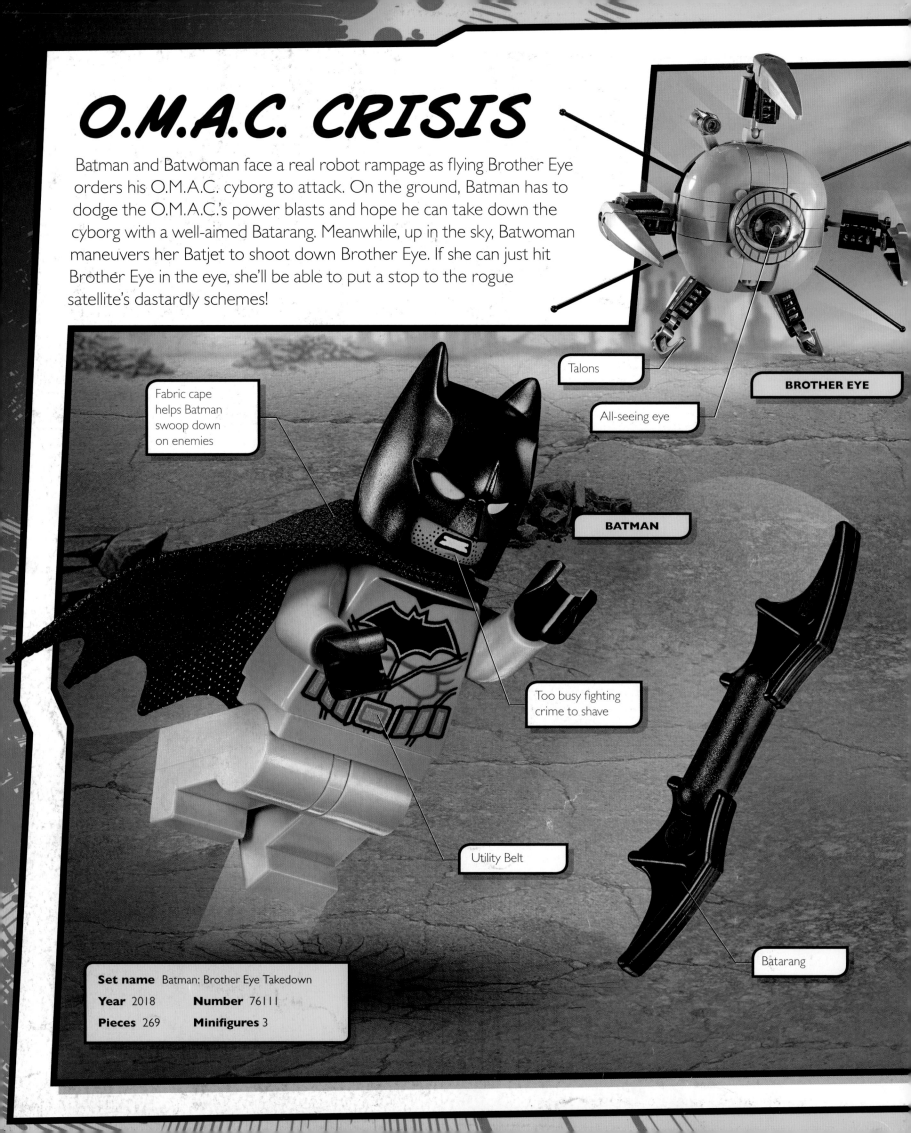

Talons

All-seeing eye

BROTHER EYE

Fabric cape helps Batman swoop down on enemies

BATMAN

Too busy fighting crime to shave

Utility Belt

Batarang

Set name Batman: Brother Eye Takedown	
Year 2018	**Number** 76111
Pieces 269	**Minifigures** 3

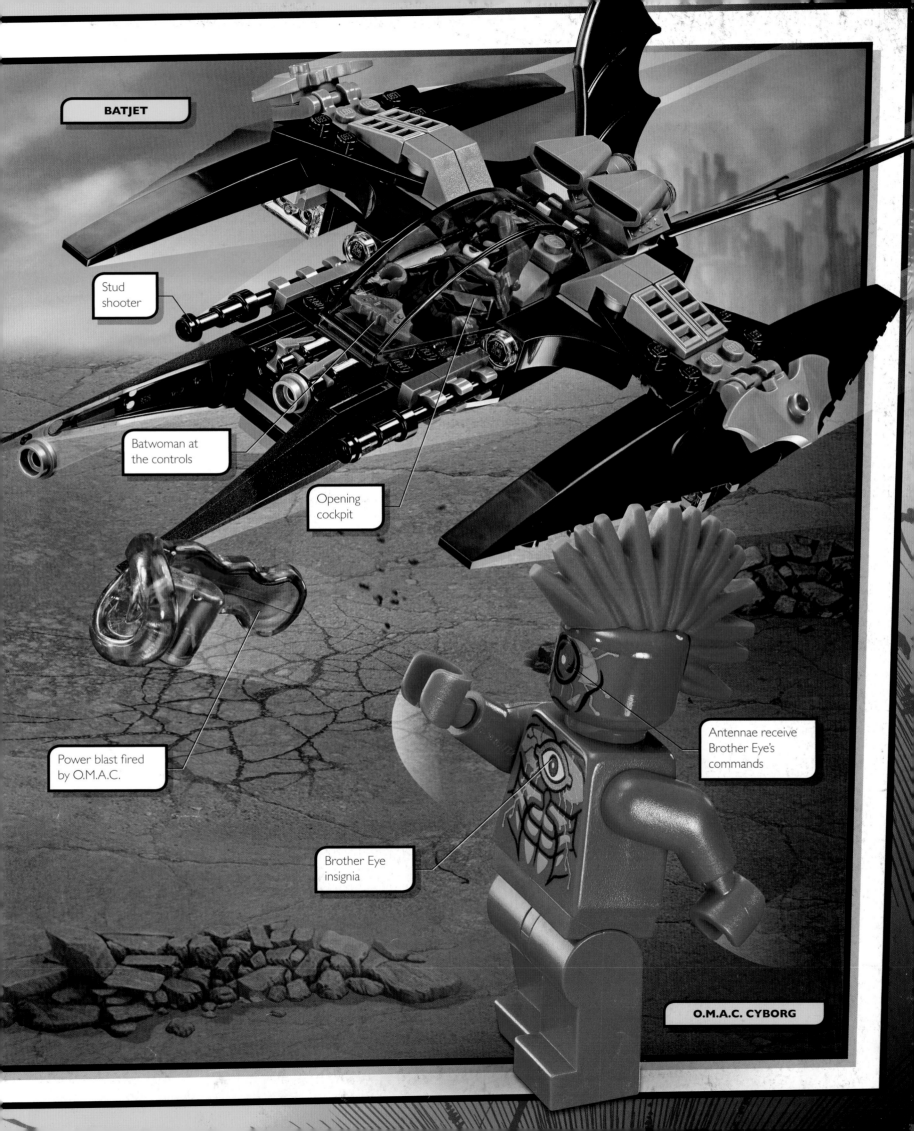

BATJET

Stud shooter

Batwoman at the controls

Opening cockpit

Power blast fired by O.M.A.C.

Antennae receive Brother Eye's commands

Brother Eye insignia

O.M.A.C. CYBORG

WATER ATTACK

Crime doesn't take place only on dry land. Luckily, Batman has a fleet of speedy water vehicles full of gadgets to help him chase down the bad guys and deliver justice out on the ocean wave. From speedboats to submarines, Batman can tackle fishy activity over and under the sea.

Harpoon

Navy-blue scuba Batsuit

Flick-fire missile

► BATMAN'S SCUBA VEHICLE

Venture under the water with Batman on his shark-shaped scuba vehicle as he chases the Penguin in the search for stolen diamonds being guarded by robotic penguins. His scuba craft is armed to the teeth and pierces through the water with an aerodynamic nose and five fins.

Set name
Batman: The
Penguin Face Off

Year 2014

Number 76010

Pieces 136

Minifigures 2

▼ BATBOAT

All aboard! This Batboat has space for Robin as well as Batman. Each hero sits in his own pod that can also break off to make a separate mini boat for speedy pursuits. The top section hinges up to reveal a radar system and console for tracking the villain Deathstroke and the diamonds he has stolen.

Section with radar dish bends up

Missiles can be aimed thanks to a ball joint

Set name The Batboat Harbor Pursuit

Year 2015   **Number** 76034

Pieces 264   **Minifigures** 3

Set name Batman: Jet Surfer (polybag)

Year 2012   **Number** 30160

Pieces 40   **Minifigures** 1

Space for cape to
billow in the wind

▶ BAT-JETSKI

Surf's up with this cool, compact build.
The one-minifigure jetski is the speediest
way to patrol and chase criminals around
the coastline. Should Batman track them
down, he can take them out with the
missiles attached to either side.

Poseable wings

Flick-fire missile

Wheel to
open engine

◀ BAT SUB

Set name
Black Manta
Deep Sea Strike

Year 2015

Number 76027

Pieces 387

Minifigures 4

The deep blue sea doesn't hold any
fear for Batman with this customized
sub that's been designed for the deepest depths.
Long and thin, the Bat Sub spears through the
water like an arrow to rescue sidekick Robin who
is being held hostage by super-villain Black Manta.

Removable
glider to help
Robin home

Water bomb
drop from the
back of the boat

▶ ARCTIC BATBOAT

Mr. Freeze is on thin ice when Batman is after him
in his all-white Arctic Batsuit and powerful Batboat.
The craft is supercharged with two water bombs
and disc missiles, making
it perfect for rescuing
Aquaman, who has
been trapped in
a block of ice
by Mr. Freeze.

Flames
shoot out
of the back

Disc missile

Set name Arctic Batman vs.
Mr. Freeze: Aquaman

Year 2013   **Number** 76000

Pieces 198   **Minifigures** 3

Blade piece

KNIGHTCRAWLER

Baddies beware the Knightcrawler! It is a huge armored tank bursting with weapons. Batman brings it out to fight against giant foe Steppenwolf and his Parademons. The Knightcrawler is deployed when Batman needs to team up with the Justice League.

► TWO TANKS IN ONE

The Knightcrawler has two different modes. It can roll on speedy double wheels that sit inside large footpads. Or, for rough terrain, it can rearrange itself to walk on small feet like a huge, four-legged spider. In this mode, the tank in the movie can even walk up walls and hang from ceilings.

Transparent-red cockpit canopy

This leg is halfway between crawling and walking mode

Treads around wheels are long LEGO® Technic beams

Rubber tires run smoothly

THE COCKPIT

Batman sits in the command seat behind a transparent-red, hexagonal canopy. His seat is built with hidden bright-yellow bricks to add a touch of Batman style.

This leg is in walking mode

Hexagonal shooters can be loaded with six stud missiles

CRAWLER

WALKER

CRAWLER TO WALKER

Just like the real Knightcrawler, the LEGO model can switch between two modes thanks to its LEGO Technic frame. Each leg has a large joint that makes it easy to reshape the leg into any position. In a moment, the Knightcrawler can switch from walking at speed to crawling over obstacles.

This leg is in crawling mode

Harpoon missile

Set name	Knightcrawler Tunnel Attack	
Year 2017		**Number** 76086
Pieces 622		**Minifigures** 4

THE BATCAVE

Hidden deep under Wayne Manor is Batman's secret headquarters—the awesome Batcave. Villainous intruders are keen to learn Batman's secrets, so the Caped Crusader and Robin the Boy Wonder must drive them away. This is the largest LEGO Batcave set and it's based on Batman's underground base from the 1960s Batman TV series.

SET HISTORY: THE BATCAVE

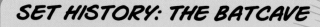

Batman and Robin have captured Poison Ivy in this Batcave set. They must fight Bane, who has come to rescue her. With a ton of Bat-gear to hand, that shouldn't be too hard!

| **Set name** |
| The Batcave |
| **Year** 2012 |
| **Number** 6860 |
| **Pieces** 689 |
| **Minifigures** 5 |

UP AND OVER

One way into the lair is up the front of the house, climbing a rope attached at the top by a grappling hook. From the roof, minifigures can drop into the study where they'll find the secret entrance.

Bat-symbol marks where the Batcopter should land

Red sticks of dynamite thrown by the Riddler

FRONT VIEW

The whole front of the tallest section is disguised as Wayne Manor

Curved shape of underground caves

Tape reel

Batcycle

Lie detector with "true" and "false" lights on top

Set name	
Batman Classic TV Series—Batcave	
Year 2016	**Number** 76052
Pieces 2526	**Minifigures** 9

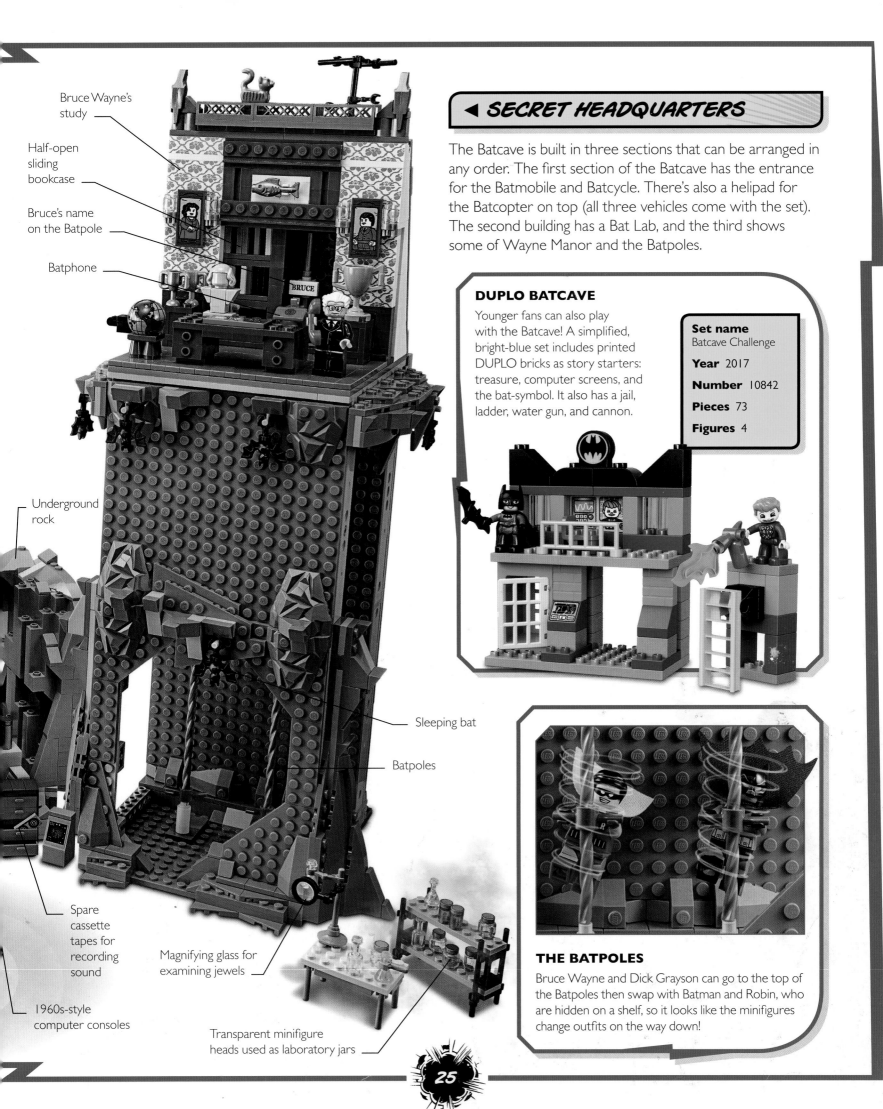

Bruce Wayne's study

Half-open sliding bookcase

Bruce's name on the Batpole

Batphone

Underground rock

Spare cassette tapes for recording sound

1960s-style computer consoles

Magnifying glass for examining jewels

Transparent minifigure heads used as laboratory jars

Sleeping bat

Batpoles

The Batcave is built in three sections that can be arranged in any order. The first section of the Batcave has the entrance for the Batmobile and Batcycle. There's also a helipad for the Batcopter on top (all three vehicles come with the set). The second building has a Bat Lab, and the third shows some of Wayne Manor and the Batpoles.

DUPLO BATCAVE

Younger fans can also play with the Batcave! A simplified, bright-blue set includes printed DUPLO bricks as story starters: treasure, computer screens, and the bat-symbol. It also has a jail, ladder, water gun, and cannon.

Set name	
Batcave Challenge	
Year	2017
Number	10842
Pieces	73
Figures	4

THE BATPOLES

Bruce Wayne and Dick Grayson can go to the top of the Batpoles then swap with Batman and Robin, who are hidden on a shelf, so it looks like the minifigures change outfits on the way down!

Pouches on Utility Belt are new for Robin

ROBIN

If you see Batman, Robin probably isn't far behind. Robin is a loyal and brave sidekick and he is the second caped crusader who makes up the Dynamic Duo with Batman. When he isn't fighting crime in his Robin costume, Robin is Dick Grayson, a friend of Batman's alter ego, Bruce Wayne.

"R" on the belt buckle

▲ SPECIAL SIDEKICK

When he is kidnapped in the desert by villain Rā's al Ghūl, Robin's minifigure has a hood to protect him from the fierce sun. He wears a short yellow cape with bat-style points. The double-sided head on this 2016 minifigure can look fierce or scared.

Robin's staff

Black mask

The only Robin minifigure not to wear a belt

MESSY HAIR
When doing battle at Jokerland, Robin's minifigure is sporting a new spiky hairstyle. His sleeves are short and he's ready for business with the stick he's carrying as a weapon.

DARKER ROBIN
Robin has a more serious look when in pursuit of Deathstroke at the harbor. He has shaggier hair, a darker red and green costume, and a black cape.

▶ REDBIRD CYCLE

Robin, in an all-red suit and black cape, matches his red-and-black motorcycle. The speedy bike is called the Redbird Cycle, and it's Robin's first vehicle of his own. The bike is based on the one Robin drives in the 1997 live-action movie *Batman & Robin*.

Robin wears an all-red suit with black trunks

Curves make the bike aerodynamic

Large wheels mean Robin can speed alongside the Batmobile

Set name	Robin and Redbird Cycle (polybag)	
Year 2013	**Number** 30166	
Pieces 40	**Minifigures** 1	

▼ THE BATCOPTER

With its own large helipad at the Batcave, this red Batcopter is based on the one flown in the 1960s movie and TV series. Robin pilots the chopper, which has a large bubble canopy and a unique bat-head-shaped print.

Long rotor blades spin

Printed bat wing on the tail rudder

Robin pilots with a control stick in each hand

Set name
Batman Classic TV Series—Batcave

Year 2016

Number 76052

Pieces 2526

Minifigures 9

Short sleeves

Laced-up tunic

Transparent red light on wing

Oversized bat wings

CLASSIC ROBIN

Robin's minifigure from the 1960s TV series wears a simple black mask and classic costume, including short green pants over bare legs.

▼ MIGHTY MICROS SPEEDY CAR

Robin's car might be small, but it's speedy against Bane and his deadly driller—not to mention his dynamite. The nimble car coordinates with Robin's trademark colors and has a special new LEGO piece for the spoiler with Robin's "R" symbol.

Grapple-hook gun

Set name Mighty Micros: Robin vs. Bane

Year 2016 | **Number** 76062

Pieces 77 | **Minifigures** 2

LITTLE ROBIN

Young Robin is mini but mighty with his short legs. A simplified Utility Belt print and cartoonish face with large eyes completes his Mighty Micros look.

Smoky windshield

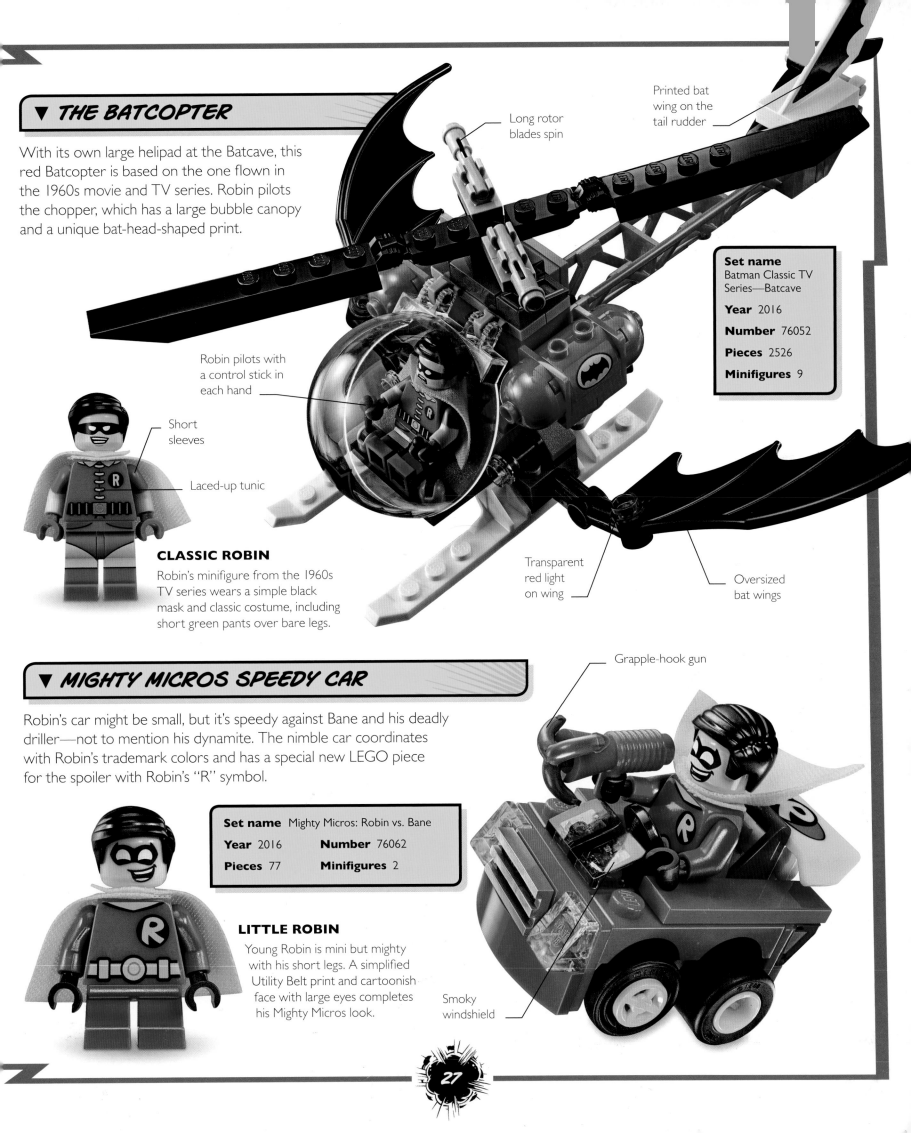

LOYAL FRIENDS

Being a Super Hero can be a lonely business, especially for Bruce Wayne, who was orphaned when he was young. Fortunately, he's found a great bunch of people to share his life as well as the burden of being Batman. Here are Batman's loyal and faithful friends and allies.

Red Batphone answered by Alfred

Smart butler's uniform

Raised eyebrow

Side part in hairpiece

◀ DICK GRAYSON

An orphan like Bruce Wayne, Dick becomes Bruce's adopted son. Also like Bruce, he adopts a secret identity when he becomes Batman's sidekick, Robin. This minifigure is based on his style in the 1960s TV show *Batman*.

▲ ALFRED PENNYWORTH

A faithful butler, Alfred has dedicated his life to serving Master Bruce Wayne. He brings order and calm to Wayne Island, keeping everything running like clockwork, whether upstairs in Wayne Manor or underground in the Batcave. Batman's secret identity is safe with Alfred!

Ordinary clothes—no one would suspect he's really Robin!

Bald head shows LEGO stud

"SWAT" stands for "Special Weapons and Tactics"

▶ COLONEL HARDY

Colonel Nathan Hardy is an officer in the U. S. Air Force. He works with Superman when the Man of Steel teams up with the military to defeat Kryptonian General Zod's attack on Metropolis.

Walkie-talkie detail

Bulletproof vest detail

▶ COMMISSIONER GORDON

James "Jim" Gordon is the police commissioner of Gotham City, working closely with Batman to fight crime. This minifigure is based on his character in the Dark Knight trilogy.

Flak jacket for protection

▶ PRISON GUARD

Upholding the law in Gotham City is no easy job, and this guard is particularly unlucky. In Arkham Asylum, dangerous prisoners break out of his jailhouse. Then, in Batmobile and the Two-Face Chase, the bank he's guarding is raided. He's just grateful that Batman and his allies are there to save the day!

Security badge clipped to pocket

Regular uniform for a security guard

Submachine gun piece

Eyes are his only facial feature

Red bat-symbol

▲ RED HOOD

The Red Hood has an uneasy relationship with the Bat-Family. Sometimes they work together well; sometimes they work against each other. Mounted on his red motorcycle—which is fitted with a machine gun—he protects Gotham City from the likes of Killer Croc and Captain Boomerang.

Long hair attached to cowl

◀ BATGIRL

Barbara Gordon wants to fight crime like her father, Commissioner Gordon, and takes the secret identity of Batgirl. In THE LEGO® BATMAN MOVIE, she becomes Gotham City's police commissioner.

Batarang

Orange Batarang

◀ BATWOMAN

Batwoman is a wealthy heiress who uses her money to fight crime. She also uses her detective skills and martial arts expertise to take matters into her own hands! Cutting-edge weapons and gadgets make her a truly formidable crime fighter.

Red cloth cape

▼ ACE THE BAT-HOUND

Bat-symbol on his collar

You don't have to chase villains on two legs to be a Batman ally. German shepherd dog Ace the Bat-Hound completes a crime-fighting trio with Batman and Robin. Clever and loyal, he has a great sense of smell and wears a mask inspired by Batman's cowl.

Utility Belt

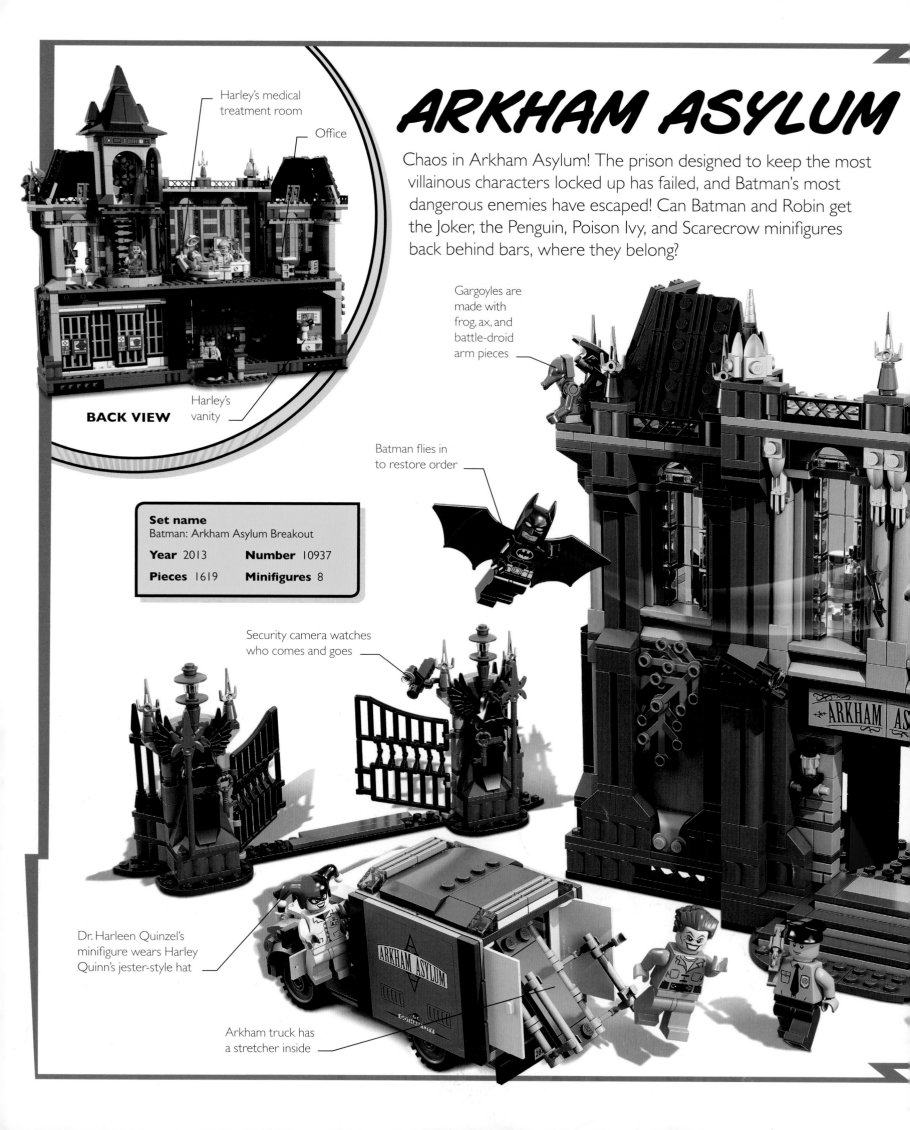

Harley's medical treatment room

Office

ARKHAM ASYLUM

Chaos in Arkham Asylum! The prison designed to keep the most villainous characters locked up has failed, and Batman's most dangerous enemies have escaped! Can Batman and Robin get the Joker, the Penguin, Poison Ivy, and Scarecrow minifigures back behind bars, where they belong?

BACK VIEW

Harley's vanity

Gargoyles are made with frog, ax, and battle-droid arm pieces

Batman flies in to restore order

Set name
Batman: Arkham Asylum Breakout

Year 2013   **Number** 10937

Pieces 1619   **Minifigures** 8

Security camera watches who comes and goes

ARKHAM AS

Dr. Harleen Quinzel's minifigure wears Harley Quinn's jester-style hat

Arkham truck has a stretcher inside

The turret houses a room with ice crystals for Mr. Freeze

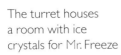

Spooky Arkham Asylum is a huge gray, gothic-style house with spires and stained glass that is built in three parts. Covered in sculptures and vines and with broken windows, it looks in a state of disrepair. Arkham has a grand, gated entrance and its own truck for transporting inmates securely—most of the time!

Mr. Freeze's attic cell

MEDICAL ROOM

In the medical treatment room, Dr. Harleen Quinzel treats sick prisoners. She is actually the villain Harley Quinn and is helping them to plot their escape!

Bricks with grooves look like grand columns

CUSTOM CELLS

Poison Ivy can control plants with her mind. She has a greenhouse-style cell with a large, transparent curved wall and vines. The bars on the window are LEGO telescope pieces!

Scarecrow escapes on a studded rope piece

Smile is the biggest on any Superman minifigure

SUPERMAN

It's a bird! It's a plane! It's Superman! The Super Hero known as the Man of Steel was born on the planet Krypton but raised on Earth. His superpowers include super-strength, super-speed, flight and heat vision. He keeps the city of Metropolis safe from super-villain Lex Luthor.

Dark blue suit

▲ MAN OF JUSTICE

Superman is mighty, but he doesn't always work alone. This 2016 minifigure clashes with Batman but also teams up with Batman and Wonder Woman to take on giant foe Steppenwolf. It's a fierce battle, and his hair ends up getting tousled.

Flat, smart hair for the office

HERO OF THE CITY

Superman faces many different villains, including General Zod, in this particular costume. This minifigure has a dark-blue suit with gold details.

TEAM PLAYER

Superman helps his Justice League friends to defeat dangerous Darkseid who is causing mayhem in the city. He wears his bright-blue suit with yellow belt.

CLARK KENT

Superman's alter ego is journalist Clark Kent. Underneath his dress shirt and messy tie, Clark's Super Hero costume is visible in this minifigure.

LEGO® DUPLO® SUPERMAN

Superman joins Batman and Wonder Woman to save the day in Gotham City. Their mission is to rescue a cat, and Superman doesn't hesitate before lifting a heavy bridge to save the kitty.

Arms are poseable

Set name
Batman Adventure
Year 2015
Number 10599
Pieces 47
Figures 3

▼ LEGO® DIMENSIONS FLIER

Superman's LEGO® Dimensions flier is one of only two vehicles he has at his disposal. He's so fast he doesn't really need help to travel quickly, but this blue-and-red flier zips around Metropolis at super speed when he needs a rest.

Hover Pod's bricks can also be used to build a Krypton Striker or a Super Stealth Pod

Set name
LEGO Dimensions: Superman Fun Pack
Year 2016
Number 71236
Pieces 48
Minifigures 1

Head has red eyes on the back

DIMENSIONS HERO

This bright-blue suited Superman has a big grin and spit-curl hair piece.

Vehicle connects to the computer for gameplay

▼ MIGHTY MICROS SUPER CAR

Superman rides a small open-topped car to face enemy Bizarro in this mini Mighty Micros set where two mini vehicles do battle. Superman can use the giant fists mounted on the front of his super car to tackle the strange super-villain.

Set name	Mighty Micros: Superman vs. Bizarro	
Year 2017		**Number** 76068
Pieces 93		**Minifigures** 2

Big fists show his super strength

Blue rudder

Unique Superman-printed tile

Lattice roof tile

SMALL SUPERMAN

The famous red-and-blue suited hero is back but with a simpler torso design. And, like in all Mighty Micros sets, he has short legs so he's just the right height for the control stick.

▼ KRYPTO THE SUPER-DOG

Krypto is a superpowered dog. Like Superman, he comes from Krypton and has similar powers—plus super determination. This corageous canine has a unique LEGO molded body, and he teams up with Superman against the alien Lobo.

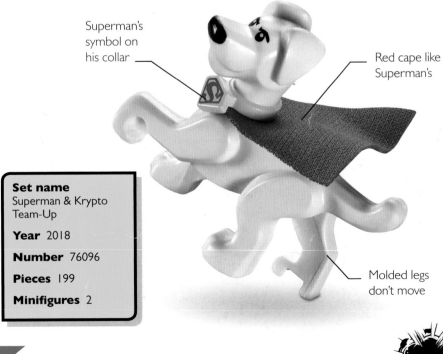

Superman's symbol on his collar

Red cape like Superman's

Molded legs don't move

Set name
Superman & Krypto Team-Up
Year 2018
Number 76096
Pieces 199
Minifigures 2

Set name	Heroes of Justice: Sky High Battle	
Year 2016		**Number** 76046
Pieces 517		**Minifigures** 5

Always on the lookout for a story, Lois carries a camera

Nice black suit for the office

▲ LOIS LANE

Fearless reporter Lois Lane works with Clark Kent at the *Daily Planet* newspaper in Metropolis. She becomes his girlfriend, and he flies to her rescue when she is kidnapped by Lex Luthor. Her minifigure wears a black suit for the office.

◀ SUPERGIRL

Born on the planet Krypton, super-strong Supergirl is now based on Earth with her cousin Superman. She can fly and has heat vision, can see through objects, and can zoom in to see microscopic details. She wears a soft cape and red boots.

Printed legs on a red leg piece leave the skirt and boots red

SUPERMAN'S FAMILY

All from the planet Krypton—or created with Kryptonian DNA—Superman's family members have super strength, speed, and stamina. His cousin, father, and a young clone form his family unit, and they all swoop in to help each other to defeat their many foes.

▼ MIGHTY MICROS SUPERGIRL CAR

Supergirl is tearing off in her mini Mighty Micros vehicle that has wheels like a car and three wings like a rocket or plane. She's clutching an enormous magnifying glass for examining the shrunken Bottle City of Kandor, which Brainiac has miniaturized and stolen.

Magnifying glass

Yellow rudder piece

Set name	
Mighty Micros: Supergirl vs. Brainiac	
Year 2018	**Number** 76094
Pieces 80	**Minifigures** 2

SUPER MIGHTY

Supergirl's Mighty Micros minifigure has short legs—and short hair. She has a cartoon-style face with a big lopsided grin. Her costume is plain, and pants allow for free movement in battle.

Pale-blue suit

Hood is similar to Superman's Mighty Micro vehicle, except the S-shield is printed the other way around

◀ JOR-EL

Jor-El is a Kryptonian scientist, but he's best known for being Superman's father. He designed the rocket that took baby Kal-El—who would become Superman—to Earth. His minifigure wears the same printed suit and cape as Superman's Man of Steel minifigure but in darker shades.

Silver print matches Superman's suit

Red version of the Superman symbol

▶ SUPERBOY

Brave Superboy is a young friend of Superman's. He is a clone, created in just a few months from a mix of Kryptonian and human DNA. His exclusive minifigure was part of a Target minifigure gift set.

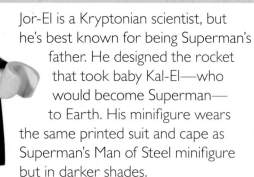

CYBORG

Cyborg was once a man called Victor Stone. After a terrible accident, his father repaired his body with cybernetics, making him part human and part machine. This gave Cyborg super strength, super speed, and physical resilience as well as the ability to repair himself. He can also interact with machines like a computer does.

Red cybernetic eye

Built-in flick-fire weapon (sonic white noise cannon)

Knee pads

◀ SUPER CYBORG

The first Cyborg minifigure battles the super-villain Darkseid alongside Superman. His armor is shiny and metallic. His double-sided head shows him happy and angry. His cybernetic helmet has a red light.

▲ JUSTICE LEAGUE CYBORG

A specially molded LEGO helmet captures Cyborg's unusual machine/human head. This 2017 minifigure also has a new arm feature: Cyborg can have a stud or an entire flick-fire gun incorporated into his body. His armor also has an updated print design in black, silver, and red.

▼ CYBORGCOPTER

Cyborg gets his wings in 2018 with a CyborgCopter for battling Killer Frost's ice car. It's a sturdy helicopter with built-in weapons including the ability to shoot a new red, circular net. Like Cyborg himself, it's gray with details in red and a shiny metallic silver.

CYBORG PILOT

For controlling his CyborgCopter, the new Cyborg minifigure has plain legs and simplified printing on his torso. His double-sided head smiles on one side and looks stern on the other.

WEAPONS

If he leaves his CyborgCopter, Cyborg doesn't go unarmed. Sections on each side of the craft clip off and can be held by a minifigure. He has two stud shooters and a radar dish that doubles as a gun.

SHOOTERS

Set name
Speed Force Freeze Pursuit
Year 2018
Number Pieces 271
Minifigures 4

Detachable shooter

Rotor blades

Net shooter

Gold tiara

WONDER WOMAN

Born on the island of Themyscira, Princess Diana is the daughter of the Amazon Queen Hippolyta. When a plane from the outside world crash-lands in her home, Diana saves the pilot. From then on, this brave warrior makes a vow to protect the world as Super Hero Wonder Woman.

Armored skirt

▼ READY FOR BATTLE

Wonder Woman is determined to uphold the Amazon cause and fight for peace. Discovering the angry war god Ares in her midst, this 2017 Wonder Woman minifigure is equiped with full Amazon battle armor—complete with weapons harness and bulletproof bracelets.

▲ AMAZON HERO

Wonder Woman teams up with the Justice League in 2016 to battle Lex Luthor and again in 2017 to face Steppenwolf and his Parademons. Her costume is a dark red and blue with gold trim and headband. She knows that working as a team is sometimes the most powerful way to take on the most fearsome foes.

Magical Amazonian shield

▼ INVISIBLE JET

Wonder Woman's 2015 Invisible Jet is one of the larger versions of the airship. But it isn't really a jet at all—it's an alien crystal that can take the form of any vehicle. With its missile launchers and ability to fly around unnoticed, it's a true wonder!

Flame exhaust

Opening cockpit

Set name	Gorilla Grodd Goes Bananas	
Year 2015	**Number** 76026	
Pieces 347	**Minifigures** 5	

Silver trimming on costume

SILVER DETAILS
In battle with Gorilla Grodd, Wonder Woman wears long trousers and a silver-trimmed costume with a silver version of her headband.

Missile launcher

Headlight

WEAPONS

SWORD

SHIELD

LASSO

Wonder Woman is highly trained in the use of swords and shields. Diana traps her foes in the Lasso of Truth, which forces those caught in it to tell the truth.

▼ ANOTHER DIMENSION

Wonder Woman pilots her LEGO Dimensions 3-in-1 Invisible Jet, which can change into a Stealth Laser Shooter or Torpedo Bomber. The versatile vehicle's hinged wings help it to fly in all directions.

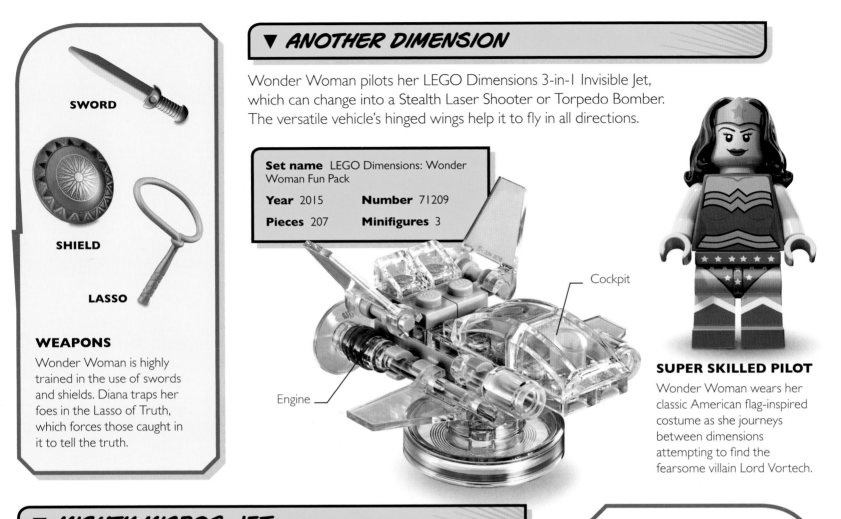

Set name LEGO Dimensions: Wonder Woman Fun Pack

Year 2015 **Number** 71209

Pieces 207 **Minifigures** 3

Cockpit

Engine

SUPER SKILLED PILOT

Wonder Woman wears her classic American flag-inspired costume as she journeys between dimensions attempting to find the fearsome villain Lord Vortech.

▼ MIGHTY MICROS JET

Riding a Mighty Micros Invisible Jet, which doubles as a car, Wonder Woman battles the monstrous Doomsday. Thanks to her vehicle's the larger tires at the back of the vehicle, Wonder Woman pops a wheelie, lurching backward and dodging Doomsday's assault.

LEGO DUPLO BIKE

While some of Wonder Woman's adventures are epic, others are smaller in scale. In order to rescue a cat in distress, Diana races to the scene on her star-spangled motorbike. To her, saving this kitty is as important as saving the world.

Set name Batman Adventure

Year 2015

Number 10599

Pieces 47

Figures 3

Set name Mighty Micros: Wonder Woman vs. Doomsday

Year 2017

Number 76070

Pieces 85

Minifigures 2

Amazonian battle shield

Vertical stabilizer

SMALL AND MIGHTY

To drive her small and mighty jet, Wonder Woman wears a cheeky grin. She knows she can outsmart Doomsday.

Tires are staggered in size

WARRIOR BATTLE

The Amazon Princess Wonder Woman must do battle with Ares, the God of War. He's a giant figure, built from bricks like a scaled-up minifigure. Wonder Woman is accompanied by American pilot Steve Trevor, who flies a vintage plane. He swoops in to help her battle the fearsome, fiery foe.

Helmet is an animal skull with poseable horns and jaws

Glowing red eyes

Enormous shield

ARES, GOD OF WAR

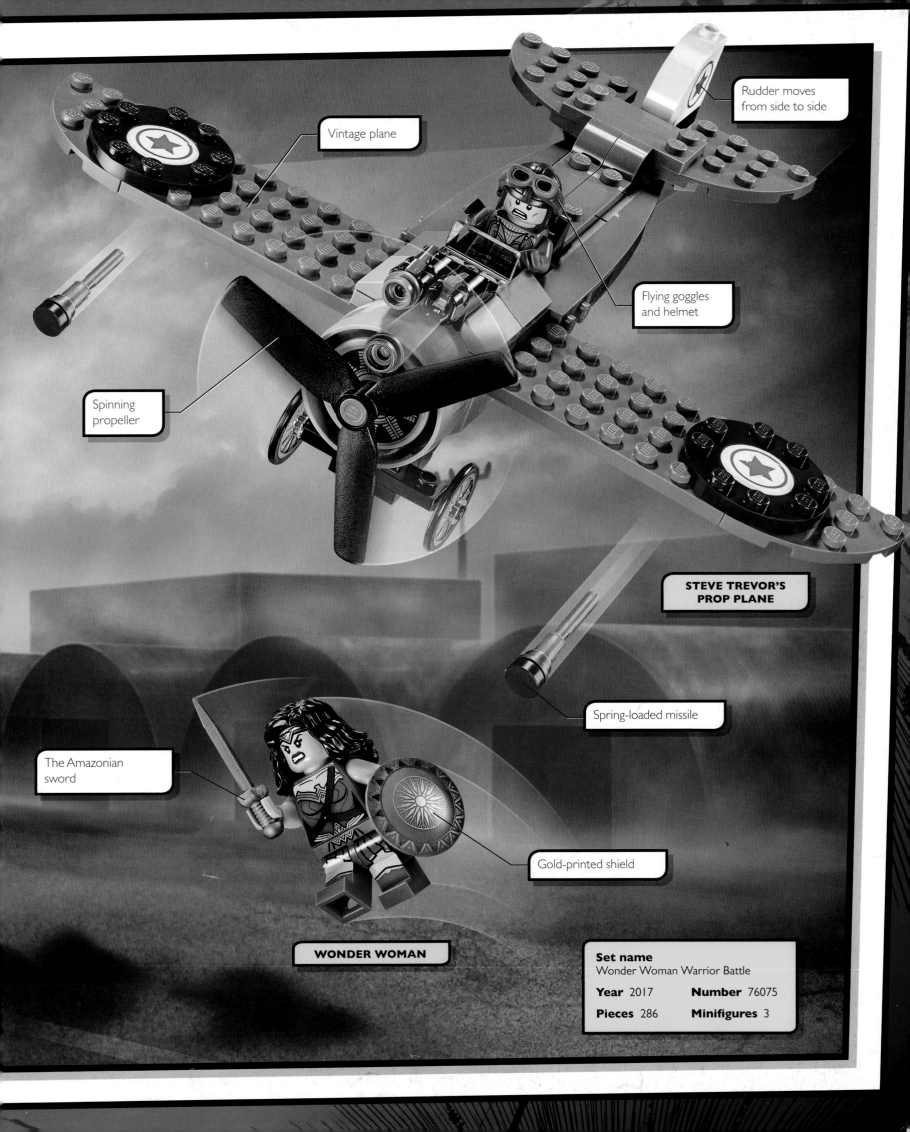

Rudder moves from side to side

Vintage plane

Flying goggles and helmet

Spinning propeller

STEVE TREVOR'S PROP PLANE

Spring-loaded missile

The Amazonian sword

Gold-printed shield

WONDER WOMAN

Set name
Wonder Woman Warrior Battle

Year 2017   **Number** 76075

Pieces 286   **Minifigures** 3

THE FLASH

There was once an easy-going guy named Barry Allen, but when an experiment went wrong during an electrical storm, he gained a superpower called Speed Force. Now he's The Flash—the Fastest Man Alive! He can manipulate Speed Force into lightning arcs and can speed-read for super fast learning.

Gold rather than yellow flash

Silver lines reflect the armored suit from the movie

▲ JUSTICE LEAGUE MEMBER

Based on his character in the 2017 *Justice League* movie, The Flash's suit is in two shades of red and has very detailed printing on both his torso and legs. His helmet's wings are small and metallic gold.

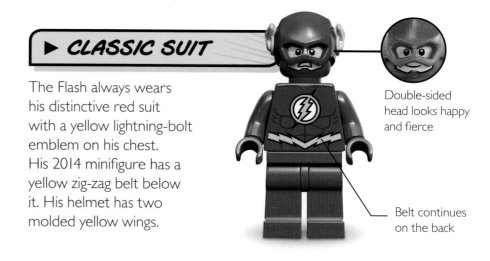

► CLASSIC SUIT

The Flash always wears his distinctive red suit with a yellow lightning-bolt emblem on his chest. His 2014 minifigure has a yellow zig-zag belt below it. His helmet has two molded yellow wings.

Double-sided head looks happy and fierce

Belt continues on the back

▼ MIGHTY MICROS CAR

In his super speedy Mighty Micros red car, The Flash zooms into battle against Captain Cold's snowplow. The Flash's secret accessory is a can of energy drink—perhaps to speed up his car rather than him! His car shoots flames out of the back.

VITAMIN DRINK

POWER BLASTS

EQUIPMENT

The Flash has yellow and blue power blasts of electricity. He also sips special vitamin drinks for an extra boost.

Set name	The Flash vs. Captain Cold	
Year 2016	**Number**	76063
Pieces 88	**Minifigures**	2

Exhaust flames

Captain Cold's snow cone

Wheels roll super fast

Yellow wheel pieces are only in Mighty Micros sets

SPEEDY FLASH

Mighty Micros mini-sized legs don't slow The Flash down! Underneath his winged helmet, his face is printed with plain white eyes and a cheekier smile.

GREEN LANTERN

If your planet's in trouble, you need a Green Lantern. There are many Green Lanterns across the universe, and each protects an area of space. Earth has former pilot Hal Jordan as its designated Green Lantern. He wears a power ring, charged by a Power Battery, which gives him the ability to create anything solid out of its green light.

Green Lantern
Corps insignia

Green boot effect
created by printing
the top of the legs

EQUIPMENT

This minifigure-held lantern isn't a weapon but a type of battery. It charges up the Green Lantern's ring, from which he gets his own power. Without it, the Green Lantern would be powerless.

POWER BATTERY

▲ PROTECTOR OF EARTH

Green Lantern's muscular minifigure wears the uniform of the Green Lantern Corps—a type of intergalactic police force. He has a green mask and wears green boots. This minifigure flies a streamlined spaceship against super-villain Sinestro.

► GREEN LANTERN'S SPACESHIP

This is the missile-packed spaceship that Green Lantern constructed for himself out of green light. He uses it to race after his archenemy, Sinestro, along with Space Batman, to retrieve his stolen Power Battery.

Stabilizer fins
can be angled

Turn the gray piece
to fire the two
front missiles

Spare ammo
for the stud
shooters stored
on the wings

Printed Green
Lantern symbol

Reclined seat for
one minifigure

Stud shooter
on each wing

Front missile is
remotely activated

Set name	Green Lantern vs. Sinestro	
Year 2015		**Number** 76025
Pieces 174		**Minifigures** 3

Spiky hair sticks straight up

NIGHTWING

Former circus acrobat Dick Grayson is a great success as Batman's famous vigilante sidekick Robin. But he decides to step out of the shadows and become a crime-fighting hero in his own right— Nightwing! He learns most of what he knows about fighting crime from Batman and is highly skilled in martial arts.

Nightwing symbol wraps around to his back

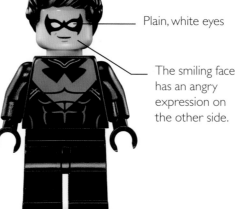

Plain, white eyes

The smiling face has an angry expression on the other side.

◀ CLASSIC SUIT

Nightwing's 2016 minifigure (polybag set 30606) dons his signature black and blue suit. He's armed with two blue Escrima sticks to match his costume and sports typically wild hair.

▲ HELPFUL HERO

Nightwing wears a black suit with red Nightwing symbol to help Batman battle furry foe Man-Bat. He has matching red eyes visible through his black mask. It's a tough battle, and his hair is very tousled!

▼ MIGHTY MICROS CAR

Nightwing races into battle against the Joker in an aerodynamic Mighty Micros car. His compact black and blue vehicle echoes the colors of his suit. The car has a steering wheel, but Nightwing is too busy waving his Escrima sticks to steer. He looks like he just wants to put his foot down!

Escrima stick is the same LEGO piece as a *Star Wars* lightsaber blade

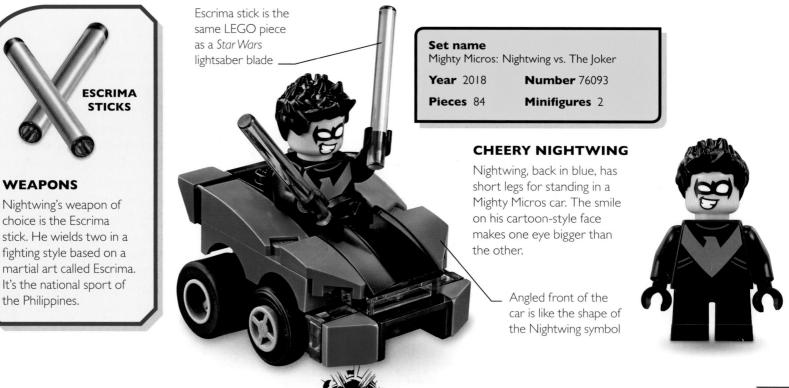

ESCRIMA STICKS

WEAPONS

Nightwing's weapon of choice is the Escrima stick. He wields two in a fighting style based on a martial art called Escrima. It's the national sport of the Philippines.

Set name	
Mighty Micros: Nightwing vs. The Joker	
Year 2018	**Number** 76093
Pieces 84	**Minifigures** 2

CHEERY NIGHTWING

Nightwing, back in blue, has short legs for standing in a Mighty Micros car. The smile on his cartoon-style face makes one eye bigger than the other.

Angled front of the car is like the shape of the Nightwing symbol

GREEN ARROW

His name tells you exactly who this Super Hero is! Green Arrow is a skilled archer who fights crime with his emerald-colored bow and arrows. Really, he's a rich businessman named Oliver Jonas Queen, but this sometime-member of the Justice League likes to don a green tunic and shoot justice from his bow.

Dark stubble

Compound bow and arrow

Golden belt buckle with an arrow

WEAPON

Unlike a basic bow, a compound bow has a levering system that gives it more power. It was produced in green specially for Green Arrow.

COMPOUND BOW

▲ ACE ARCHER

Green Arrow's outfit draws inspiration from his name. This minifigure uses three shades of green for his tunic and trousers, with detailed printing to show the texture of the fabric. He wears his hood down, revealing bright yellow hair.

▼ THE JAVELIN

Green Arrow pilots the Justice League's ship, the Javelin, to protect Metropolis from the villainous Darkseid on his Hover Destroyer. The Javelin has a surprise. Minifigures can hide and then spring from the rear of the ship with a super jumper function, operated by a red ball on a lever.

Under the two shell pieces is a compartment with two seats for minifigures and the super jumper function

Pressing this gray tile opens the main compartment

Set name	
Darkseid Invasion	
Year	2015
Number	76028
Pieces	545
Minifigures	4

Black lever moves the wings into landing mode

Wings in flying mode

BATMAN'S ALLIES

Batman often works alone, but sometimes he teams up with other heroes to get the job done. As a defender of justice all over the world, Batman has many allies, including members of the Justice League, the Outsiders, and the Teen Titans.

Three prongs

TRIDENT OF POSEIDON

WEAPON

Aquaman uses his trident to create magical energy and force fields to help him defeat his enemies. It can control water and create storms.

▼ AQUAMAN

Aquaman, is half human and half Atlantean. Split between two worlds, he has sworn to protect both of them—life on land, and life underwater in Atlantis. His powers include telepathic power over marine life.

Printed scales and muscles on his torso

Scales on green pants

▼ MERA

Mera is a princess from Xebel and she's also the Queen of Atlantis. She can manipulate the density of water and change it into objects. Mera is married to fellow Super Hero, and Batman ally, Aquaman.

Shaggy eyebrows

Trident of Poseidon

Trident creates giant waves, storms, whirlpools and even earthquakes

Fish scales

Red hair

Blue power blast element

Scales printed on aqua colored costume

AQUA HERO

This Aquaman minifigure wears dark colors and has long shaggy hair. He carries the magical Trident of Poseidon.

THE ORIGINAL

Aquaman's original minifigure has bright clothing that reflects his bold comic book costume. His trident is gold.

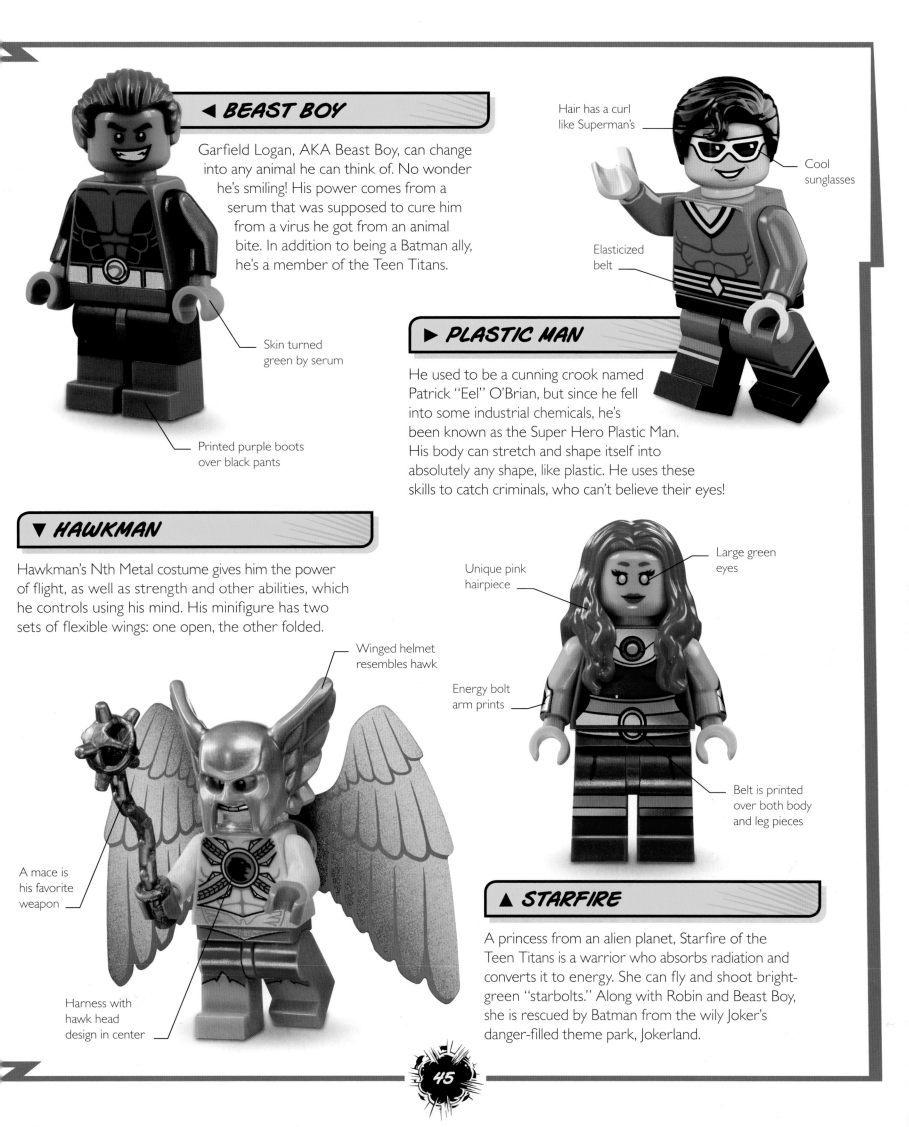

◄ BEAST BOY

Garfield Logan, AKA Beast Boy, can change into any animal he can think of. No wonder he's smiling! His power comes from a serum that was supposed to cure him from a virus he got from an animal bite. In addition to being a Batman ally, he's a member of the Teen Titans.

Skin turned green by serum

Printed purple boots over black pants

Hair has a curl like Superman's

Cool sunglasses

Elasticized belt

► PLASTIC MAN

He used to be a cunning crook named Patrick "Eel" O'Brian, but since he fell into some industrial chemicals, he's been known as the Super Hero Plastic Man. His body can stretch and shape itself into absolutely any shape, like plastic. He uses these skills to catch criminals, who can't believe their eyes!

▼ HAWKMAN

Hawkman's Nth Metal costume gives him the power of flight, as well as strength and other abilities, which he controls using his mind. His minifigure has two sets of flexible wings: one open, the other folded.

Winged helmet resembles hawk

A mace is his favorite weapon

Harness with hawk head design in center

Unique pink hairpiece

Large green eyes

Energy bolt arm prints

Belt is printed over both body and leg pieces

▲ STARFIRE

A princess from an alien planet, Starfire of the Teen Titans is a warrior who absorbs radiation and converts it to energy. She can fly and shoot bright-green "starbolts." Along with Robin and Beast Boy, she is rescued by Batman from the wily Joker's danger-filled theme park, Jokerland.

HEROIC ALLIES

Super Heroes have all kinds of amazing powers, but it's tough to save the world all by yourself. Fortunately, there's a network of like-minded heroes out there who have each other's backs. Whether on their own or in groups, these heroes have plenty to offer!

Unique LEGO armor piece has two small wings

Power element

▲ BLUE BEETLE

Jaime Reyes becomes a member of the Teen Titans after he bonds with a robotic blue scarab. It gives him living blue armor that creates weapons and gadgets, boosts his physical powers, and allows him to fly.

► STEVE TREVOR

Pilot goggles

U.S. Air Force pilot Steve Trevor is a close friend of Wonder Woman. His minifigure wears a vintage pilot outfit. It's a uniform with old-fashioned flight goggles that fit over his helmet.

Ribbed sweater

High boots

◄ LIGHTNING LAD

Lightning flash detail

Superman ally Lightning Lad fizzes with electricity, which he can manipulate. He's also a founder of the young Legion of Super Heroes team. The back of his head shows him with red eyes, generating electrical blasts.

Gloves protect against accidental electric discharges

► SHAZAM!

Lightning flash

When Billy Batson says "Shazam!" he's transformed into a Super Hero. He's a Justice League ally, and he also passes magical powers onto his friends, the Shazam! Family.

White version of Superman's cape

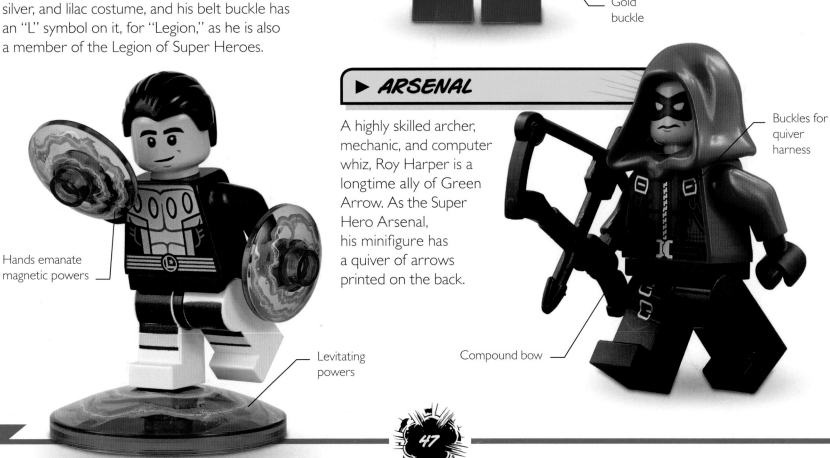

Clear hand grip holds energy bolt

Flame pieces

◀ FIRESTORM

Firestorm's nuclear power is conveyed by glowing transparent LEGO pieces. This Justice League hero has flames shooting from his feet, power bolts and blasts firing from his hands, and flames blazing from his head piece.

Power burst

Lines reveal the shape of his face

◀ MARTIAN MANHUNTER

J'onn J'onzz, the Martian Manhunter, has fought crime alongside the Justice League using his amazing shape-shifting and telepathic powers. His unique blue collar is a small, cape-style piece.

Gold buckle

▼ COSMIC BOY

Cosmic boy is from the planet Braal. He has magnetic powers, like everyone from his planet. He uses his powers to help the Justice League battle super-villains. Cosmic Boy wears a black, silver, and lilac costume, and his belt buckle has an "L" symbol on it, for "Legion," as he is also a member of the Legion of Super Heroes.

Hands emanate magnetic powers

Levitating powers

▶ ARSENAL

A highly skilled archer, mechanic, and computer whiz, Roy Harper is a longtime ally of Green Arrow. As the Super Hero Arsenal, his minifigure has a quiver of arrows printed on the back.

Buckles for quiver harness

Compound bow

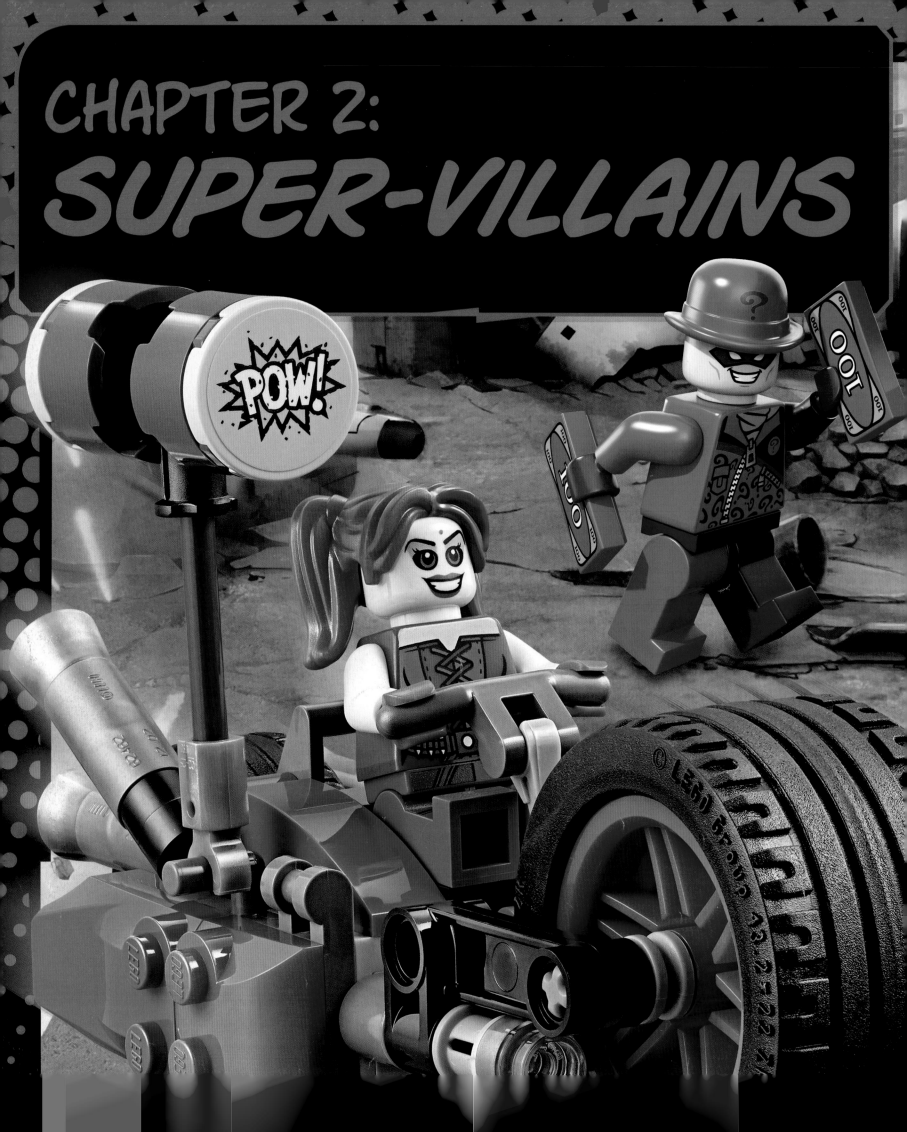

CHAPTER 2: SUPER-VILLAINS

Smile shows
yellow teeth

THE JOKER

He's the feared underworld kingpin with seaweed-green locks, a red rictus grin, and a fondness for purple clothes. He is the Joker—the Batman's greatest nemesis. The clown prince of crime continually matches wits with the Dark Knight, hoping to someday stump his brilliant foe.

Detailed blue
checkered
waistcoat

▲ JOKERLAND CLOWN

This manic minifigure from 2015 is a circus of printed detail, from his checkered blue waistcoat and sickly green bow tie to his orange shirt and purple jacket. The Joker may know how to pull off a heist, but he does not know how to color coordinate!

DARK NIGHT FOE

This minifigure is a morbid masterpiece. His face has a natural skin tone buried under white makeup, his smile is painted on, and his dual-sided head reveals rotting teeth.

ARKHAM ENEMY

The Joker wears his Arkham Asylum uniform. This jumpsuit has an elaborate belt buckle. The back is printed with his inmate number (109370)—nearly his set number (10937)!

CRIMINAL CLOWN

This Joker minifigure, based on the classic 1960s Batman TV show, has a mustache! The stripe detail on his pants continues on the sides of his legs, giving him a retro look.

▼ ROLLICKING ROLLER

The Joker's steamroller is coming! Get out of the way! This clownish construction concoction has a spiked orange roller that can swivel from side to side. As if that wasn't enough, it's got flickable laughing gas bombs that look like clown faces, capped off with round red LEGO® stud noses.

Trick gun with
"Bang" flag

Buildable "grinning
mouth" façade

Set name	Batman: The Joker Steam Roller	
Year	2014	Number 76013
Pieces	486	Minifigures 5

HENCHMAN

Even the Joker's henchmen look like circus folk! This fearsome fellow has a removable hard hat and crowbar to complete his loony look!

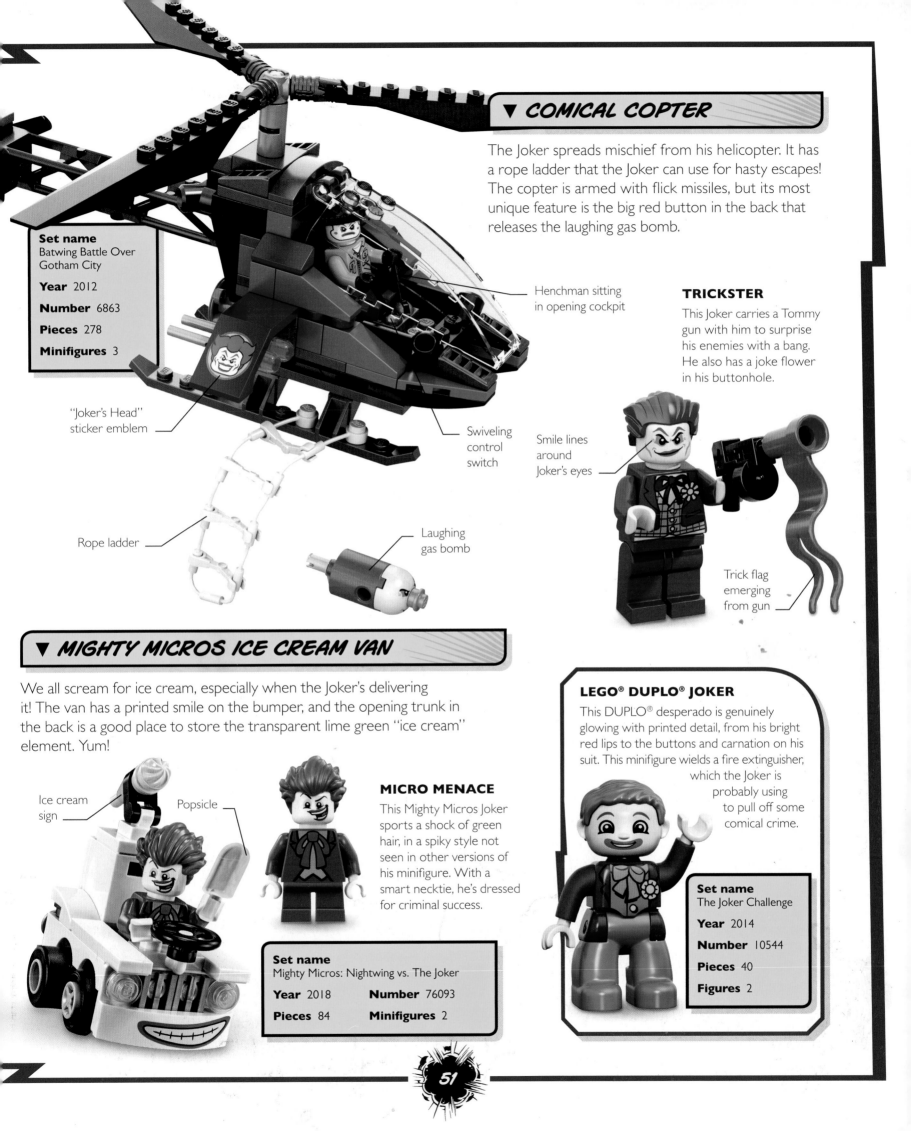

▼ COMICAL COPTER

The Joker spreads mischief from his helicopter. It has a rope ladder that the Joker can use for hasty escapes! The copter is armed with flick missiles, but its most unique feature is the big red button in the back that releases the laughing gas bomb.

Set name
Batwing Battle Over Gotham City

Year 2012

Number 6863

Pieces 278

Minifigures 3

Henchman sitting in opening cockpit

"Joker's Head" sticker emblem

Swiveling control switch

Rope ladder

Laughing gas bomb

TRICKSTER

This Joker carries a Tommy gun with him to surprise his enemies with a bang. He also has a joke flower in his buttonhole.

Smile lines around Joker's eyes

Trick flag emerging from gun

▼ MIGHTY MICROS ICE CREAM VAN

We all scream for ice cream, especially when the Joker's delivering it! The van has a printed smile on the bumper, and the opening trunk in the back is a good place to store the transparent lime green "ice cream" element. Yum!

Ice cream sign

Popsicle

MICRO MENACE

This Mighty Micros Joker sports a shock of green hair, in a spiky style not seen in other versions of his minifigure. With a smart necktie, he's dressed for criminal success.

Set name
Mighty Micros: Nightwing vs. The Joker

Year 2018   **Number** 76093

Pieces 84   **Minifigures** 2

LEGO® DUPLO® JOKER

This DUPLO® desperado is genuinely glowing with printed detail, from his bright red lips to the buttons and carnation on his suit. This minifigure wields a fire extinguisher, which the Joker is probably using to pull off some comical crime.

Set name
The Joker Challenge

Year 2014

Number 10544

Pieces 40

Figures 2

JOKERLAND

The Joker and his villainous cronies have taken Gotham City's greatest amusement park and turned it into the horrendous Jokerland. Robin, Beast Boy, and Starfire are trapped inside! Will Batman fall prey to Jokerland's terrifying traps and silly snares? Or will he rescue his friends from this carnival of convicts?

Batman enters Jokerland in his Batmobile, which boasts an opening cockpit, spring-loaded missiles, and rear stud shooters. The Joker holds court from his podium in the mouth of a clown's head with rolling eyes. He also has a robot clown who wields a ball-firing cannon!

THE PENGUIN'S DUCK RIDE

The Penguin's ride features rotating duck seats that are crammed with dynamite! Beast Boy ejects Penguin using the ride's Super-Jumper-activated toppling function!

Harley's high-wire bike

Duck seat filled with dynamite

Fires spring-loaded missiles

Set name	
Jokerland	
Year	2015
Number	76035
Pieces	1037
Minifigures	8

Tilting hat

Push the sign to
activate Poison
Ivy's ride

CARNIVORE
FREE
FALL!

Slide into
toxic vat

TOXIC
TANK

Fires cannonballs

SHOOT 'O' MATIC

POISON IVY'S BIG DROP

Poison Ivy has trapped Robin, Beast Boy and
Starfire in her ride, which features a plant with
snapping jaws! One push on the "Free Fall" sign
and the heroes plunge down into the toxic vat.

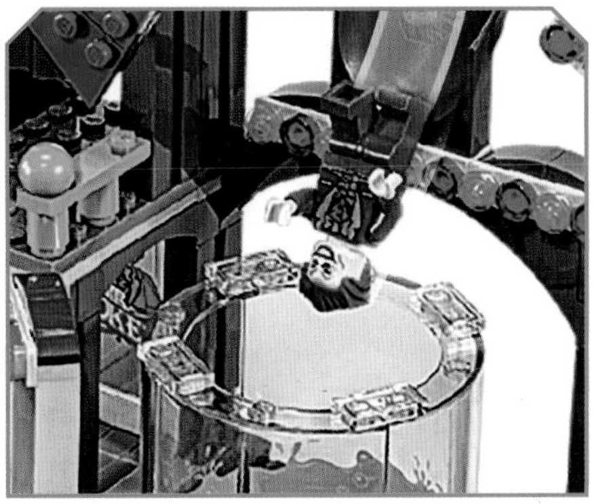

SLIME DUNK

A slide leads from the clown's head to
the vat of toxic slime! Push down on the
clown's tongue and the Joker slides into
the toxic tank.

SET HISTORY: FUN HOUSE

In this 2012 set, the Joker, the Riddler,
and Harley Quinn hold Robin hostage
in their evil fun house.

Set name
Dynamic Duo
Funhouse Escape

Year 2012

Number 6857

Pieces 380

Minifigures 5

Top hat

Dapper purple pants

THE PENGUIN

Oswald Cobblepot grew up being mocked for his appearance and his waddle. But nobody mocks him now that he's the gangster known as the Penguin! Always impeccably dressed, the Penguin wears a top hat and a tuxedo. He always carries one of his gadget-laden umbrellas, which doubles as a weapon.

◀ 1960S PENGUIN

This minifigure from 2016 is based on the Penguin seen in the classic 1960s Batman TV series. Whereas other versions of the Penguin minifigure have black hats, this version has a purple hat.

▲ ELEGANT ENEMY

The Penguin always dresses to impress, and it shows in this minifigure that was first released in 2013. Details include his monocle and striped waistcoat. He wears elegant white gloves on his hands. Even his purple mini-legs match his bow tie!

▼ DANGEROUS DUCK BOAT

The Penguin's duck boat might look cute and harmless, but looks can be deceiving! If you need proof, check out the flick missiles under each wing. A propeller in the back provides power for the vehicle, which the Penguin controls using the steering wheel inside.

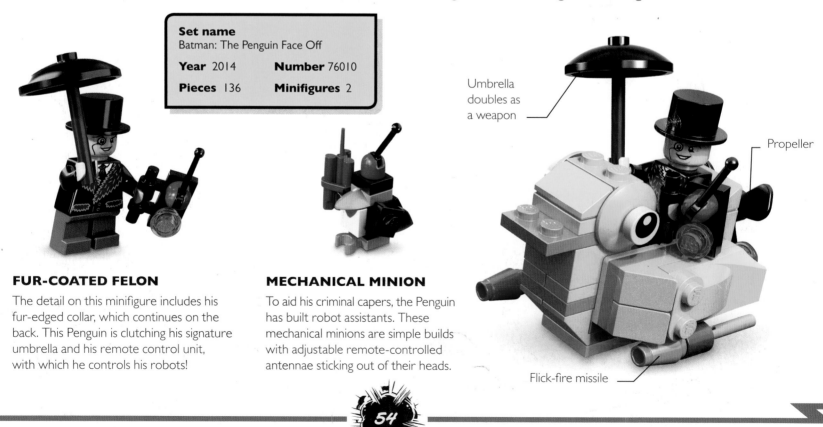

Set name	
Batman: The Penguin Face Off	
Year 2014	**Number** 76010
Pieces 136	**Minifigures** 2

Umbrella doubles as a weapon

Propeller

FUR-COATED FELON

The detail on this minifigure includes his fur-edged collar, which continues on the back. This Penguin is clutching his signature umbrella and his remote control unit, with which he controls his robots!

MECHANICAL MINION

To aid his criminal capers, the Penguin has built robot assistants. These mechanical minions are simple builds with adjustable remote-controlled antennae sticking out of their heads.

Flick-fire missile

CATWOMAN

Cat burglar Selina Kyle just can't resist the lure of a thrilling caper! She's an accomplished gymnast with a sneaky skill for stealing jewels. Often she's a thorn in Batman's side, but sometimes she teams up with the Dark Knight and helps the heroes of Gotham City.

Mask doubles as Catcycle helmet

Printed detail on belt

▶ CATCYCLE

Catwoman leaps astride her Catcycle. There's an in-built grip for her whip, and the kickstand is raised so she can strike a classic pose. This the perfect little getaway vehicle for a jewelry store robbery!

Transparent diamond element

Set name	
Catwoman Catcycle City Chase	
Year 2012	**Number** 6858
Pieces 89	**Minifigures** 2

▼ MIGHTY MICROS CAT CAR

Catwoman has stolen a carton of milk and a diamond, and she's escaping in her Mighty Micros car! The vehicle sports a cat-face design in the front with printed cat eyes and cat ears flanked by the headlights. Between the taillights, there's an adjustable cat's tail.

Set name	
Mighty Micros: Batman vs. Catwoman	
Year 2016	**Number** 76061
Pieces 79	**Minifigures** 2

Stolen milk carton

Headlight

MINI KITTY

This micro-sized minifigure even has a belt with a cat's-head clasp. She's wearing purple lipstick for a quirky look!

▲ FELINE FELON

The torso of this Catwoman minifigure from 2012 is bursting with detail, including a zipper and patterned belt. She has a menacing grimace, but a turn of her double-sided head reveals a mischievous smirk—the face of someone hoping to get away with it.

1960s hairstyle

Black whip

▲ CLASSIC CRIMES

Catwoman's 1960s Batman TV series minifigure from 2016 has cat ears that are attached to her hairband. She wears a gold necklace, and her head turns to reveal a mask and a big smile.

Bowler hat with question mark insignia

Two-tone green on arms

THE RIDDLER

Master thief Edward Nygma is obsessed with puzzles and riddles. He can't help leaving a trail of clues, which helps Batman foil his crimes. Nobody knows why the Riddler does this. It's a big question mark, like the one on the Riddler's hat!

Jacket exclusive to set

Removable money bags filled with cash

Set name Batman: The Riddler Chase

Year 2014

Number 76012

Pieces 304

Minifigures 3

▲ CRYPTIC CRIMINAL

The Riddler chuckles, waving bundles of stolen cash! He wears a green racing jacket with a question mark motif, which is also printed on his back. A purple mask conceals his identity when he's out of costume.

Exhaust pipes shoot orange flames

"Hot rod" version of logo

Supercharged engine

▲ DEVIOUS DRAGSTER

The Riddler's dragster is perfect for lightning-fast getaways. It's also equipped with a bomb launcher! This crime car is decorated with the Riddler's question mark logo surrounded by flames, giving it a classic "hot rod" look.

Lighter hair

Detailed muscle printing

Yellow question mark belt buckle

TV TRICKSTER

This minifigure is based on the Riddler from the 1960s *Batman* TV show, who sported a distinctive lilac cummerbund. Turn his head and his impish grin becomes an angry snarl.

BOWLER BADDIE

This is the first Riddler minifigure to wear a bowler hat. It looks like he's been working out, judging from the muscles showing through his green suit!

TWO-FACE

Gotham City District Attorney Harvey Dent could always see both sides of a court case, until a gangster scarred his face. Now, as crime boss Two-Face, he still sees both sides of any situation. He just flips a silver dollar to decide whether to do the right or wrong thing!

Scarred side shows furious expression

Stick of dynamite

Set name	The Batmobile and the Two-Face Chase		
Year 2011		Number 6864	
Pieces 531		Minifigures 5	

▶ DOUBLE TROUBLE

Two-Face plots his latest crime, flipping his coin, as always. His two-colored suit reflects his dual personality and continues on his back.

Split-colored suit

Safe opens to reveal money

Two-Face's silver dollar

Trying hard to look tough and streetwise

Flick-fire missiles

Crane swivels on rotating plate

Laser cannon

HARVEY'S HENCHMAN

Two-Face has two henchman to help do his dirty work. Both wear two-tone jackets in Two-Face's favorite colors and black beanies.

Bullet holes

◀ BANK ROBBERY

Two-Face is escaping in his getaway car! Using its crane, he's stolen a bank safe filled with cash. Pursuers beware— this vehicle packs some powerful weapons!

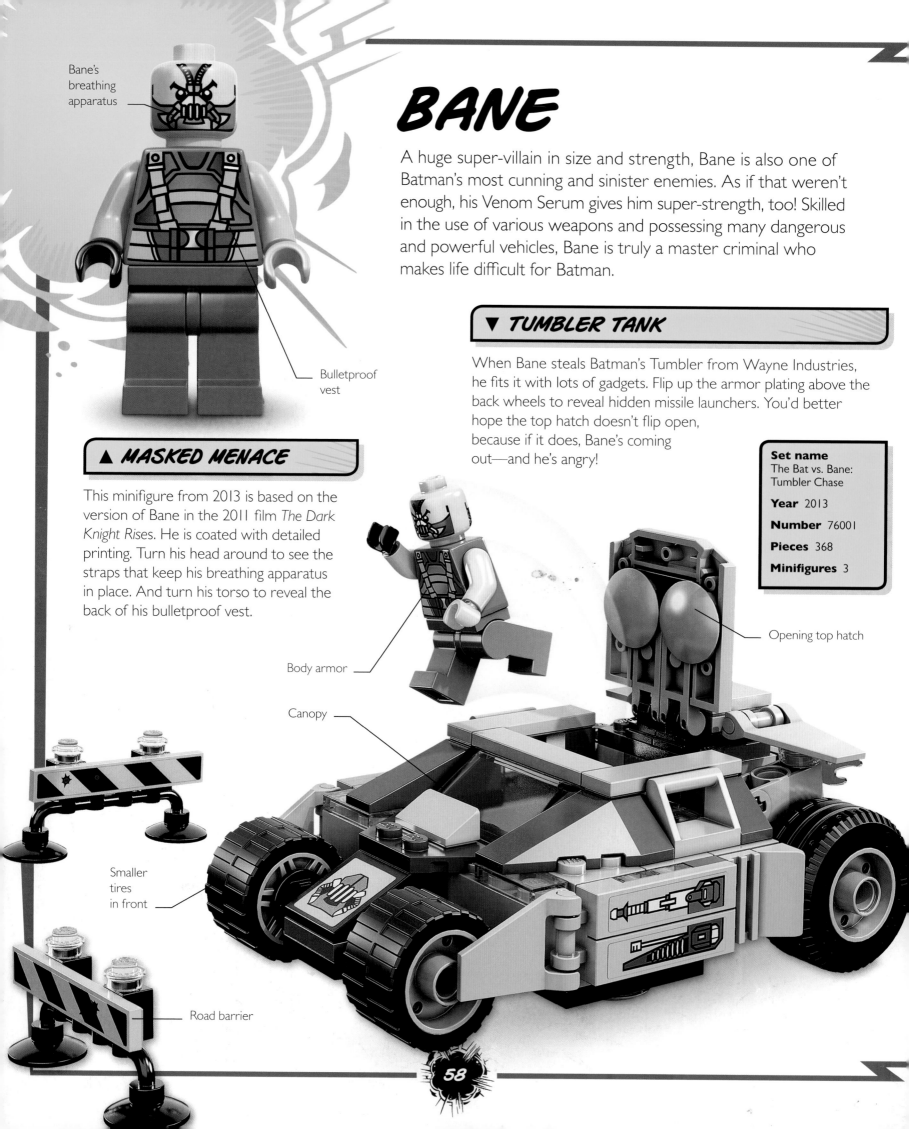

Bane's breathing apparatus

Bulletproof vest

BANE

A huge super-villain in size and strength, Bane is also one of Batman's most cunning and sinister enemies. As if that weren't enough, his Venom Serum gives him super-strength, too! Skilled in the use of various weapons and possessing many dangerous and powerful vehicles, Bane is truly a master criminal who makes life difficult for Batman.

▼ TUMBLER TANK

When Bane steals Batman's Tumbler from Wayne Industries, he fits it with lots of gadgets. Flip up the armor plating above the back wheels to reveal hidden missile launchers. You'd better hope the top hatch doesn't flip open, because if it does, Bane's coming out—and he's angry!

Set name
The Bat vs. Bane: Tumbler Chase

Year 2013

Number 76001

Pieces 368

Minifigures 3

▲ MASKED MENACE

This minifigure from 2013 is based on the version of Bane in the 2011 film *The Dark Knight Rises*. He is coated with detailed printing. Turn his head around to see the straps that keep his breathing apparatus in place. And turn his torso to reveal the back of his bulletproof vest.

Body armor

Canopy

Opening top hatch

Smaller tires in front

Road barrier

▼ DANGEROUS DRILLER

Bane's Drill Tank is great at boring tunnels, but that's the only "boring" thing about it! This vehicle features a rotating drill and flick missiles. The burrowing tank rolls ahead using its six wheels to turn its giant caterpillar tracks!

Lamp

Rotating drill

Flick missile

Caterpillar tracks

BRAWNY BAD GUY

Covering the whole of Bane's head is a mask that lets him inhale his Venom Serum. The printing on his front torso shows his black vest and huge muscles!

Head fully encased in mask

Set name	The Batcave	
Year 2012	**Number** 6860	
Pieces 690	**Minifigures** 5	

▼ MIGHTY MICROS DRILL TANK

Riding his Mighty Micros drill tank, Bane shakes an angry fist at the world around him! This vehicle is topped with a shiny spinning drill part. Orange transparent "flame" elements burst from the exhaust pipes, adding some major menace to this micro machine!

Vest has a "B" for Bane

Transparent lamp element

Exhaust with transparent flame element

Set name	Mighty Micros: Robin vs. Bane
Year 2016	**Number** 76062
Pieces 77	**Minifigures** 2

SMALL BUT MIGHTY

Mighty Micros Bane may be small, but he has plenty of attitude! He has the same mini legs as Mighty Micros Batman.

Drill bit

Unique red and blue hair piece

Ammo belt full of bullets

HARLEY QUINN

Harley Quinn was once Dr. Harleen Quinzel, the Joker's therapist at Arkham Asylum. Instead of curing her prankster patient, she dubbed herself "Harley Quinn" and joined the Joker on his comedic crime spree. From that point on, she took her place as one of Gotham City's villainous VIPs!

▲ FUNNY FELON

With a pair of pigtails replacing her signature jester's cap, Harley is letting her hair down! Harley's 2016 minifigure is printed with plenty of detail, including a lace-up red and blue corset with bullet storage.

FUNHOUSE QUINN

This 2012 Harley Quinn minifigure has lots of black and red printed diamond detail. She is grinning about holding Robin hostage in the Funhouse.

JOKERLAND JESTER

Harley causes mayhem in Jokerland in 2015. She wears short pants, and her necklace is a string of bells, so she can always be the "bell" of the ball!

HARLEEN QUINZEL

Dr. Quinzel might look like an ordinary doctor, but her super-villain costume is visible under her lab coat! The other side of her head has her Harley Quinn face!

Removable mallet attached to side

Adjustable exhaust

▼ HARLEY'S BIKE

Harley's bike has huge tires to help her escape from Batman who is in hot pursuit. The crazy bike has a mechanical hammer to bash any heroes who get too close!

▼ MIGHTY MICROS CAR

Riding a Mighty Micros car, Harley Quinn sticks her tongue out at Batman. The car is red and blue, which matches Harley's two-tone hair and outfit. Topping off the vehicle is an oversize wind-up key.

Mallet matches car's color scheme

Cheeky expression

Wind-up key piece

Set name
Mighty Micros: Batman vs. Harley Quinn

Year 2018

Number 76092

Pieces 86

Minifigures 2

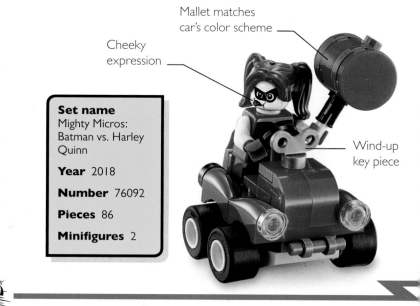

Set name
Batman: Gotham City Cycle Chase

Year 2016 **Number** 76053

Pieces 224 **Minifigures** 3

SCARECROW

Dr. Jonathan Crane is an authority on phobias. Teased and ignored by his family and friends, Crane is bitter and decides to spread fear all over Gotham City. Wearing a creepy scarecrow costume and whipping up a batch of fear gas, he makes his victims' nightmares come to life!

— Raggedy face mask

Set name
Batman: Scarecrow
Harvest of Fear

Year 2016

Number 76054

Pieces 563

Minifigures 5

Rope belt

Patches, like on real scarecrow

▶ FEAR AND FRIGHT

The Scarecrow has arrived in Gotham City, and he won't leave until he's scared more than just crows! This Scarecrow minifigure is the creepiest yet. He's oozing with detail, from his patchwork face mask to his knotted rope belt. His hat is even crooked—much like the Scarecrow himself!

Green tank of fear gas

Hose leading to gas tank

◀ SCARECROW'S HARVESTER

The Scarecrow's Harvester is carefully designed to scare Super Heroes. Its green transparent tank of fear gas opens up to capture minifigure prisoners. A detachable fear gas stud shooter hangs on the vehicle's side.

Transparent neon green propeller blade

Rotating cutters

▶ EERIE ENEMY

This 2013 minifigure is printed with visible seams and scuff marks, making him truly look like a scarecrow who's come alive! His tattered attire continues on the back of his minifigure, completing his all-around creepy look.

BATMAN'S FOES

Think about the huge number of gadgets and weapons that Batman possesses. Take that number and double it—that's how many enemies he has! Batman's foes range from wacky crooks to manic mainiacs. They all have one thing in common—a desire to defeat the Dark Knight!

Leaves adorn hair

Outfit made of leaves

Green pants for ease of movement escaping Arkham

▼ MAN-BAT

Biologist Kirk Langstrom created a serum that turned him into Man-Bat—a humanoid bat! Man-Bat is not particularly thrilled about his transformed condition, which has given him fur and wings. If you turn his revolving headpiece, you will see his worried expression.

Removable ears attached to hairpiece

Wings move with arms

▲ POISON IVY

Pamela Isley, AKA Poison Ivy, can control plants—and people—with her mind. She much prefers plants over people and is the bitter enemy of anyone who threatens her beloved greenery. Her favorite color is green, which is why she rocks green makeup. She may look friendly, but her vines can be poisonous.

Bazooka shoots LEGO studs

Removable jetpack

► DEADSHOT

Sharpshooter Floyd Lawton never misses his mark. This minifigure has a stud-shooting bazooka and jetpack accessory, to help Deadshot do his dirty work with ease. Deadshot's entire body is printed with his armored suit. His legs are printed with knee guards, and his arm printing reveals wrist-mounted guns.

Body armor and helmet keeps him cold

Ice Gun

Boomerang emblem

Boomerang

Bandolier strap full of boomerangs

◀ MR. FREEZE

Scientist Victor Fries is particularly coldhearted toward Batman, whom he blames for the lab accident that caused his chilly condition. As a result, Mr. Freeze has to wear a special suit to survive. His favorite weapon is his Ice Gun, which can freeze anyone stiff!

▲ CAPTAIN BOOMERANG

Australian criminal George "Digger" Harkness has an arsenal of boomerangs. Captain Boomerang's hat and belt buckle sport his "boomerang" emblem, while the detail on his minifigure includes a bandolier strap chock-full of boomerangs. Every time Batman defeats him, this crook always comes back—just like a boomerang!

▼ RĀ'S AL GHŪL

Rā's al Ghūl is the founder of the League of Assassins. His revolving head is printed with two faces. One has wrinkles and gray hair. The other shows him looking much younger, after he's bathed in a Lazarus Pit, which extends his lifespan by many years. Rā's has been a villain for centuries!

"Old" version of face

Ceremonial League of Assassins cape

Long, black hair

Gold shaft with blade

▶ TALIA AL GHŪL

Much like her father, Rā's, Talia al Ghūl is a master of combat and martial arts. She is equipped with a golden scythe blade. Her dark-red suit is elegant, and her revolving head reveals an angry glare.

Dark-red suit matches lipstick

Bald head

LEX LUTHOR

He is a powerful billionaire with access to all sorts of technology and weapons. He is a master inventor and calls himself the "greatest criminal mind of our time!" Meet Lex Luthor—Superman's archenemy. Obsessed with defeating the Man of Steel, Luthor constantly comes up with schemes to destroy his alien adversary.

Green and purple color scheme

◄ TYRANNICAL TAKEDOWN

Luthor strikes a powerful pose in this 2018 minifigure. This minifigure's torso printing shows off his suit's dazzling details, such as the hexagonal power pack printed on his chest. The warsuit follows Luthor's signature green and purple color scheme.

Set name	
Superman vs. Power Armor Lex	
Year	2012
Number	6862
Pieces	207
Minifigures	3

▼ POWERFUL MECH

Lex Luthor is walking tall in his Kryptonite-powered mech. It has moveable fingers and thumbs, as well as an enormous Kryptonite gun. Luthor sits in the suit's control seat, protected by a clear dome.

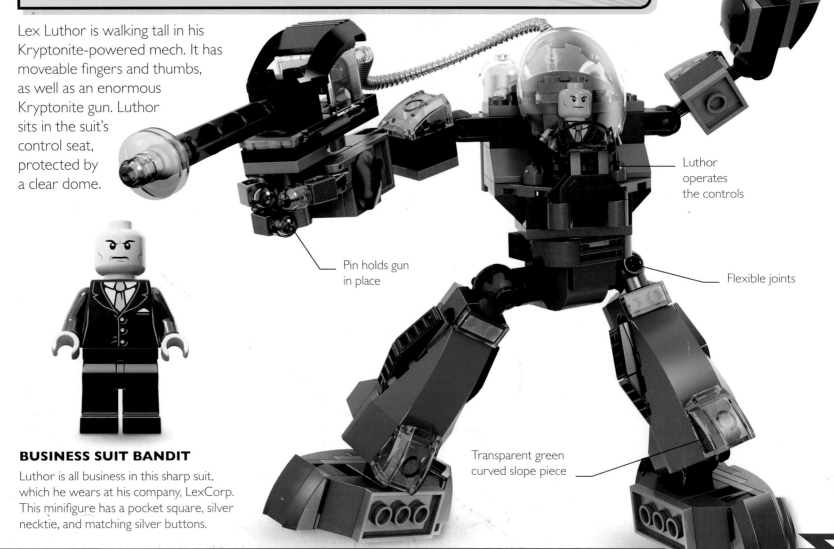

Luthor operates the controls

Pin holds gun in place

Flexible joints

Transparent green curved slope piece

BUSINESS SUIT BANDIT

Luthor is all business in this sharp suit, which he wears at his company, LexCorp. This minifigure has a pocket square, silver necktie, and matching silver buttons.

Spinning
top rotor

Spinning
rear rotor

► LEXCORP COPTER

This LexCorp helicopter, based on the 2016 film
Batman v Superman: Dawn of Justice, is as slick as
its owner, Lex Luthor. It features Kryptonite flick
missiles, a spinning rotor, and an opening cockpit.
Resourceful reporter Lois Lane grabs onto the
attachment point underneath the vehicle!

LexCorp logo

Lois Lane

Set name	
Heroes of Justice: Sky High Battle	
Year 2016	**Number** 76046
Pieces 517	**Minifigures** 5

LEISURE SUIT LEX

This minifigure is based on the version of
Lex Luthor from the 2016 film *Batman v
Superman: Dawn of Justice*. He's peppered
with printed detail, including his sand-
colored leisure suit. And this is the only
Luthor minifigure with a hairpiece.

► LEXCORP FORKLIFT

One of Luthor's henchmen is using a forklift to
move a shipment of Kryptonite crystals! This
vehicle is equipped with flick missiles, and its
movable forks allow
you to pick up the
green gemstones.
And push down
the panel in the
rear to eject
the henchman
from the
driver's seat!

Luthor's
henchman

Shipment of
Kryptonite

LEXCORP
LACKEY

Luthor's henchman
is one tough helper.
He wears his Lexcorp
ID badge and a gray
goatee beard. He
has worked for Lex
for a long time!

LexCorp jacket

Set name	
Kryptonite Interception	
Year 2016	
Number 76045	
Pieces 306	
Minifigures 3	

UNIFORMED
UNDERLING

Don't mess with this
henchman because he
wields a stud-shooting
bazooka rifle! He
wears a green LexCorp
jacket. Turn his head to
reveal his furious face.

MECH TAKEDOWN

Superman's archenemy Lex Luthor has built himself a fearsome mech, which is fueled by power units. Lex is backed up by super-villain ally Cheetah, and it's up to the Justice League to stop them both. Can Batman, Wonder Woman, and Firestorm capture the power units, shut down Luthor's mech, and save the day?

Two stud missiles

Yellow light-style elements

Transparent Power Bursts

BATMAN'S BAT-GLIDER

Batarang

Lasso of Truth

Spear

Tiara

Green power unit

WONDER WOMAN

THE CHEETAH

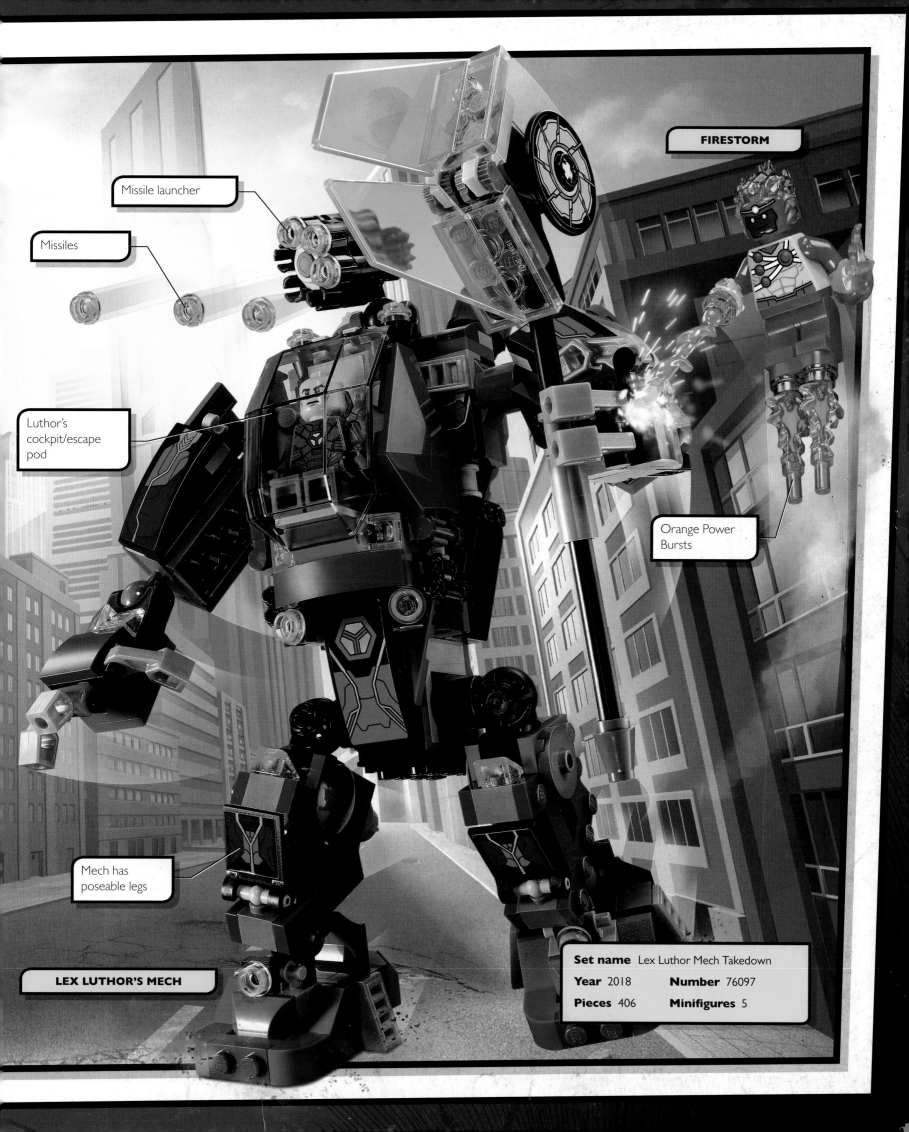

Missile launcher

Missiles

Luthor's cockpit/escape pod

Mech has poseable legs

LEX LUTHOR'S MECH

Orange Power Bursts

Set name	Lex Luthor Mech Takedown	
Year 2018		**Number** 76097
Pieces 406		**Minifigures** 5

DARKSEID

Darkseid is a being of huge power and strength. He's also the ruler of the gloomy, fiery planet Apokolips. His glowing red eyes fire Omega Beams that can destroy almost anything or teleport a target anywhere he wishes. Darkseid has tried to invade Earth several times, but, so far, the planet's Super Heroes have defeated his schemes.

Eyes launch Omega beams

Hands project blasts of energy

◄ POWERFUL FIGURE

Teeth clenched, Darkseid is a huge, scary sight. Printing on this towering figure's face and chest shows the cracks in his gray skin, as though he's ready to burst. His huge hands are specially molded to clutch his weaponry. If you see him coming, flee!

► HOVER DESTROYER

Darkseid's Hover Destroyer is just as fearsome as he is! Darkseid stands at the control platform and grabs on to the cannonball shooter. An extra cannonball is always at the ready just behind the shooter and anti-gravity discs keep the vehicle hovering just above ground so it can speed above any terrain.

Set name	Darkseid Invasion
Year	2015
Number	76028
Pieces	545
Minifigures	4

CANNONBALL SHOOTER

Darkseid's cannonball shooter tilts up and down, which makes it easy to aim. Just squeeze the top and bottom half of the shooter to fire!

Cannonball shooter

Hand on control stick

Anti-gravity disc

DEATHSTROKE

Slade Wilson used to be a marine. Now he's a villain known by the code name Deathstroke, and he is the world's deadliest assassin. His senses of sight, hearing, and smell are far greater than those of ordinary human beings, and he can heal extra-fast from wounds. He is also skilled with all kinds of weapons. Deathstroke is certainly a fearsome foe!

Orange and black mask

Ammo belt

Pouches to store gear and weapons

SWORD

PISTOL

WEAPONS

Deathstroke is an expert with all forms of weaponry. He's frequently seen wielding, and he sometimes uses a double-barreled pistol. Double the danger for his enemies!

▲ DANGEROUS VILLAIN

The detailed printing on Deathstroke's minifigure features equipment pouches on his belt. A bandolier strap, loaded with shells, wraps around his back. He wears a large black patch over one side of his face covering one of his eyes that was once badly injured.

► JETBOAT

Deathstroke is escaping from his latest heist in this jetboat! This criminal craft has two flick torpedo missiles. A gun and a sword are stashed in weapon holders. The jetboat is chained to a safe filled with diamond elements—Deathstroke's ill-gotten gains!

Exhaust

Weapons holder

Missile launcher

Jetboat with opening cockpit

Flick torpedo missiles

Set name		
The Batboat Harbor Pursuit		
Year 2015		**Number** 76034
Pieces 264		**Minifigures** 3

KILLER CROC

Reptilian powerhouse Waylon Jones prowls the Gotham City sewers, appearing only to create mayhem with his hulking frame and sharp fangs. Only Batman can stop this cold-blooded criminal, but even the Dark Knight sometimes finds it difficult to defeat Killer Croc!

Big gripping hand

Ripped blue printed shorts

Feet attach to Battle Chomper

◄ SEWER SMASHER

Killer Croc's big figure from 2017 features a unique head mold, which has a sharp-toothed smile and furrowed brow. The printed detail extends to his torso, which has scales on his muscular chest.

Lookout tower has boomerang shooter

Mouth chomps when wheels turn

► BATTLE CHOMPER

Killer Croc's Battle Chomper has movable jaws, and when the wheels turn, the mouth munches. As the vehicle moves, its hinged tail swerves around. The Battle Chomper is topped off with a lookout tower for Croc's pal Captain Boomerang. The tower even has a flick-fire boomerang shooter!

Set name
Batman: Killer Croc Sewer Smash

Year 2016	**Number** 76055	
Pieces 759	**Minifigures** 5	

Hinged swiveling tail

KILLER MOTH

Killer Moth copies Batman, possessing martial arts skills and high-tech equipment. He has imitated the Caped Crusader by creating a headquarters called the Mothcave, a vehicle called the Mothmobile, and a device called the Moth-Signal! But instead of fighting crime, Killer Moth commits crimes!

Unique molded lime green helmet

Cocoon gun

Leg printing continues on sides

WEAPON

Killer Moth's cocoon gun shoots a stream of sticky threads that covers his victims. This weapon is made from a silver ray gun attached to a transparent purple radar dish.

COCOON GUN

▲ MENACING MOTH

Colorful criminal Killer Moth has taken flight! His helmet comes off to reveal a double-sided head. One side has goggles and a calm expression; the other has no goggles and looks a bit alarmed!

▼ MIGHTY MICROS MOTHMOBILE

This villainous vehicle is shaped like a moth. The car has a LEGO drinking glass resembling an insect's mouth, the headlights have insect-eye printing, and the sides are decorated with transparent, insect-style wings. Buzzzz!

Helmet has soft rubber antennae

Stud-shooting gun

Set name	Mighty Micros: Batman vs. Killer Moth	
Year 2017	**Number** 76069	
Pieces 83	**Minifigures** 2	

"Killer Moth" emblem on chest

MIGHTY MOTH

The Mighty Micros Killer Moth minifigure has a removable lime green helmet with soft rubber antennae, and his removable transparent wings are bright orange. He wields a stud-shooting gun, which makes him a formidable foe!

CAPTAIN COLD

Leonard Snart was a thief who was captured by The Flash. Snart was resourceful and crafty and he invented a gun that could emit a blast of cold air, imprisoning his enemies in a block of ice. He became the super-villain Captain Cold. Nobody can stop him— not even The Flash!

Parka with printed detail

Transparent ice-blue "freeze" element

▲ COOL CUSTOMER

Captain Cold is snug in his blue and white parka, which is a blizzard of cool printed detail. The parka printing continues on the minifigure's back. His head turns to reveal a frosty frown! Meanwhile, his ice-blue "freeze ray" elements help his gun to do its chilling thing!

WEAPON

FREEZE GUN

Captain Cold's freeze gun can stop anyone in their tracks! Made from a classic round LEGO brick capped with a double-barreled "space gun" piece, this weapon is as cool as Captain Cold himself!

▼ MIGHTY MICROS SNOWPLOW

Captain Cold charges forth in his Mighty Micros Snowplow. This tundra-themed transporter boasts bone-chilling features, such as turning wheels and transparent ice elements. While Captain Cold zooms forth in his snowplow, he holds his freeze gun in one hand and a snow cone in the other!

Snow cone

Telescope LEGO piece

Plow

Freeze gun

Set name Mighty Micros: The Flash vs. Captain Cold	
Year 2016	**Number** 76063
Pieces 88	**Minifigures** 2

MIGHTY MICRO

This Mighty Micros Captain Cold minifigure is small in stature but has a big personality with his expressive facial printing. He packs a pint-sized punch in his cozy, fur-trimmed parka.

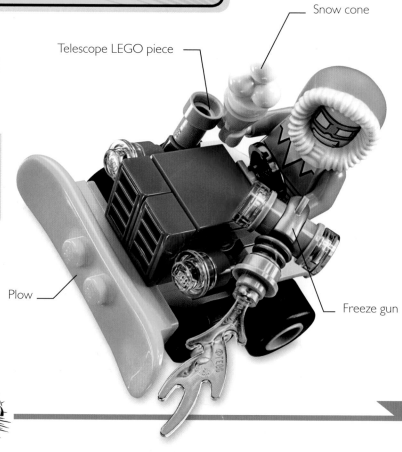

STEPPENWOLF

Steppenwolf is a military leader from an alien world. He first came to Earth many millennia ago to try to rule the planet. However, a resistance force made up of the mightiest warriors of the time defeated him, and he retreated. Now he has returned with his dreaded Parademons. Can anyone stop him?

Helmet molded on to head piece

Battle-ax

Printed detail of body armor

► COSMIC COMBATANT

Look out—Steppenwolf is on the attack! This big figure's torso is printed with his bonelike armor. Steppenwolf wields his battle-ax thanks to a clip in his right hand, and he can assume a number of combat-ready poses thanks to ball joints in his elbows, knees, hips, and shoulders.

Hand grips weapon

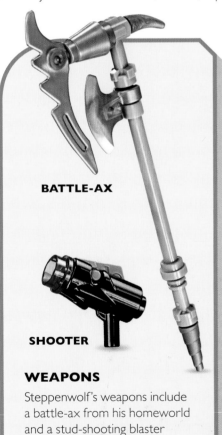

BATTLE-AX

SHOOTER

WEAPONS

Steppenwolf's weapons include a battle-ax from his homeworld and a stud-shooting blaster used by his Parademons.

► PARADEMON PALS

Steppenwolf's scary minions, the Parademons, attack from above! These minifigures' bodies are printed with bony body armor. Their interchangeable insect-style wings are very detailed. But don't let the wings distract you from their stud-shooting blasters! ZAP!

Bonelike metallic exoskeleton

Printed detail of insectlike wings

Body armor on knee

Electrodes
on front
and back
of head

Purple wires
continue
on back

BRAINIAC

Alien criminal Brainiac is a living supercomputer from the planet Colu. He is so curious about other worlds and civilizations that he roams the galaxy, visiting planets. He then shrinks their major cities with his shrinking ray and places them in bottles. Over the years, he has assembled a unique, interplanetary collection of miniature cities!

▲ COMPUTER TYRANT

Cold, calculating Brainiac is plotting his next move! A trio of pink electrodes on both sides of his head, and purple wiring is on both sides of his torso, hint at his mechanized insides.

▼ MIGHTY MICROS UFO

Clutching the bottled Kryptonian city of Kandor, Brainiac pilots his Mighty Micros UFO spacecraft, distinguished by a hinged bubble canopy and a printed "skull-face" bumper.

"UFO"-style
saucer design

Hinged opening
bubble canopy

▼ SKULL SHIP

Brainiac's scary, skull-shaped ship hovers over its prey. It has an opening cockpit, a computer screen, flick missiles, detachable laser cannons, and tentacles that swivel back and forth.

White skull
face

Hose attached
to laser cannon

Swiveling
tentacles

Set name
Brainiac Attack

Year 2015

Number 76040

Pieces 179

Minifigures 4

Set name
Mighty Micros:
Supergirl vs. Brainiac

Year 2018

Number 76094

Pieces 80

Minifigures 2

LOBO

This intergalactic bounty hunter has many names. Some call him The Main Man, some The Last Czarnian, but most know him as Lobo. Born with an accelerated healing factor, Lobo is super-strong and almost invulnerable. He has a fearsome reputation but lives by a strict code of honor and never breaks his word.

Removable hairpiece

Muscular physique

Leather pants

BOMB DROP

Push in the central green power burst at the back of the vehicle and a bomb drops out of the cargo hold!

▶ THE MAIN MAN

Just as Lobo is a unique specimen of alien life, his minifigure is a unique specimen of printed detail. He has a chain necklace, a biker jacket with multiple zippers, and a skull-shaped belt buckle. He tops off this threatening outfit with a wicked grin!

▼ SPACE HOG

Lobo's Space Hog bike is customized with Kryptonite stud shooters and adjustable booster engines. Green "power burst" elements show that Lobo is zooming through the galaxy. The nose cone looks like a skeleton with fangs.

"Energy infuser" canister

Adjustable booster engine

Stud shooter

Bomb held in undercarriage

Set name		
Superman & Krypto Team-Up		
Year 2018		**Number** 76096
Pieces 199		**Minifigures** 2

Adjustable booster engine

KRYPTONIANS

Before the planet Krypton exploded, military leader General Zod tried to overthrow the Kryptonian Council and establish himself as that world's ruler. He and his allies Faora and Tor-An were defeated and imprisoned in the Phantom Zone until Krypton's destruction, which freed them!

▼ GENERAL ZOD

Fiercely committed, General Zod won't let anything stop him from achieving his goals. This minifigure wears a cape, and his family crest is printed in silver on his chest. A twist of Zod's revolving head reveals his "heat vision" eyes!

Muscle definition

▼ KRYPTONIAN DROPSHIP

The Phantom Zone villains' Black Zero Dropship is ready to invade! This alien airship features an opening cockpit, an enormous rotating underside cannon, gigantic flick missiles, hinged storage bays, and a weapons rack! Can this dropship help Zod and his followers get the drop on Superman?

Nose cone is radar dish

Tor-An pilots the dropship

Rotating underside cannon

Set name	Superman: Battle of Smallville	
Year 2013	**Number** 76003	
Pieces 418	**Minifigures** 5	

► FAORA

Faora is Zod's second-in-command. Like Zod, she has a removable cape. She carries a Kryptonian gun, although with her superpowers, she doesn't need it! If she's happy, turn her two-sided head to reveal her grin.

Spiky black hair

► TOR-AN

Tor-An is a member of the Kryptonian Warrior Guild and he has mastered several different forms of combat. His black uniform is similar to those of his fellow Kryptonians Zod and Faora. He pilots their Black Zero dropship vehicle.

Kryptonian family crest

BLACK MANTA

Seafaring scoundrel Black Manta wants to rule the underwater world, and he'll fight anyone who stands in his way. In his quest for maritime domination, he plunders the depths for undersea treasures. Black Manta has no superpowers, but his specially made scuba suit can blast electric bolts and shoot eyebeams.

Harpoon-style spear

Helmet lets him breathe underwater

Wings

Detailed printing on torso

Transparent red cockpit

▲ MANIC MANTA

Black Manta's minifigure features the details of his scuba suit, which is also printed on his back. His helmet has bright red eyes, which feature a nice splash of detail. And air is fed into the helmet via his oxygen tubes. But beware Black Manta's harpoonlike spear!

Stud shooter

"Black Manta" symbol

▲ SEA SAUCER

Black Manta's Sea Saucer is on the move! The undersea vehicle features an eerie transparent red opening cockpit, stud shooters, and a spinning rear propeller. Because Black Manta likes to maintain an ominous vibe, the white studs on his missiles glow in the dark!

Torpedo lasers

◄ ROBOSHARK

This cyborg fish is controlled by Black Manta and is armed with torpedo launchers. Like the weapons on the Sea Saucer, Roboshark's lasers have elements that glow in the dark!

Set name	Black Manta Deep Sea Strike	
Year	2015	Number 76027
Pieces	387	Minifigures 4

FREAKY FOES

The LEGO DC Super Heroes Rogues Gallery includes the very worst criminals in the entire galaxy. Some of these super-villains are gods. Some are monsters. Others are just plain angry and up to no good! Here are some of the most memorable bad guys the LEGO DC Super Heroes have battled—and defeated—during their thrilling adventures.

Skull-shaped helmet

Legs swivel back and forth

◀ ARES

The God of War Ares is a major foe of Wonder Woman. This giant brick-built minifigure has red eyes printed on a curved, black LEGO piece. His hands have pins to hold his sword and shield in place. His torso is covered with stone-plated armor.

Blue mask printed on face

Belt pouches for tricksy equipment

Checkered pattern continues on both sides

Removable snow-white hair piece

▶ KILLER FROST

Scientist Caitlin Snow has a frosty alter ego, a chilling criminal who shoots ice from her fingers. An assortment of transparent, ice-blue "Power Burst" elements helps Killer Frost hurl bolts of ice at her enemies, particularly Firestorm. Rotate her head to reveal a snowy smirk. Cool!

"Snowflake" motif

▲ TRICKSTER

Teenager Axel Walker, the Trickster, uses gadgets and practical jokes to commit crime and annoy The Flash. His belt-and-harness printing continues on his back, where there are even more pouches for him to store his gizmos. If his hair looks unique, it's no trick! It's because no other minifigure has hair that exact color.

◄ SINESTRO

Sinestro used to be the greatest Green Lantern of them all. Now he's the Green Lantern Corps' greatest enemy! Turn his double-sided bright pink head to see him snarl as only the leader of the Sinestro Corps can!

Sinestro Corps symbol

Mind-control equipment

► THE CHEETAH

Archaeologist Barbara Minerva's cheetah powers of speed and agility help her to steal valuable artifacts. Printed detail depicts her fangs and spots, for a true, big-cat look. She's a ferocious foe to Wonder Woman.

Glamorous hairstyle

Arms swivel up and down

Printing shows off her muscles

▲ GORILLA GRODD

Gorilla Grodd is a big enemy of The Flash. He's super-intelligent, he can control minds, and he wants to conquer the world with his gorilla army! The printing on his minifigure's head reveals his gritted teeth and his glowing mind-control equipment.

Face has a confused, puzzled look

◄ BIZARRO

Scientist and villain Lex Luthor created this mixed-up clone of Superman. Bizarro needs the stone medallion around his neck to remember his own name! Detailed printing shows this muddled monster's chalky, wrinkled skin and reverse Superman symbol.

Reversed S-shield logo

► BATZARRO

Bizarro, the imperfect clone of Superman, made a clone of Batman, called Batzarro! Batzarro may look a lot like Batman, but he does exactly the opposite of what the hero would do. Even his Utility Belt and bat-symbol are on upside down.

Cape has rips and holes

Upside-down bat-symbol

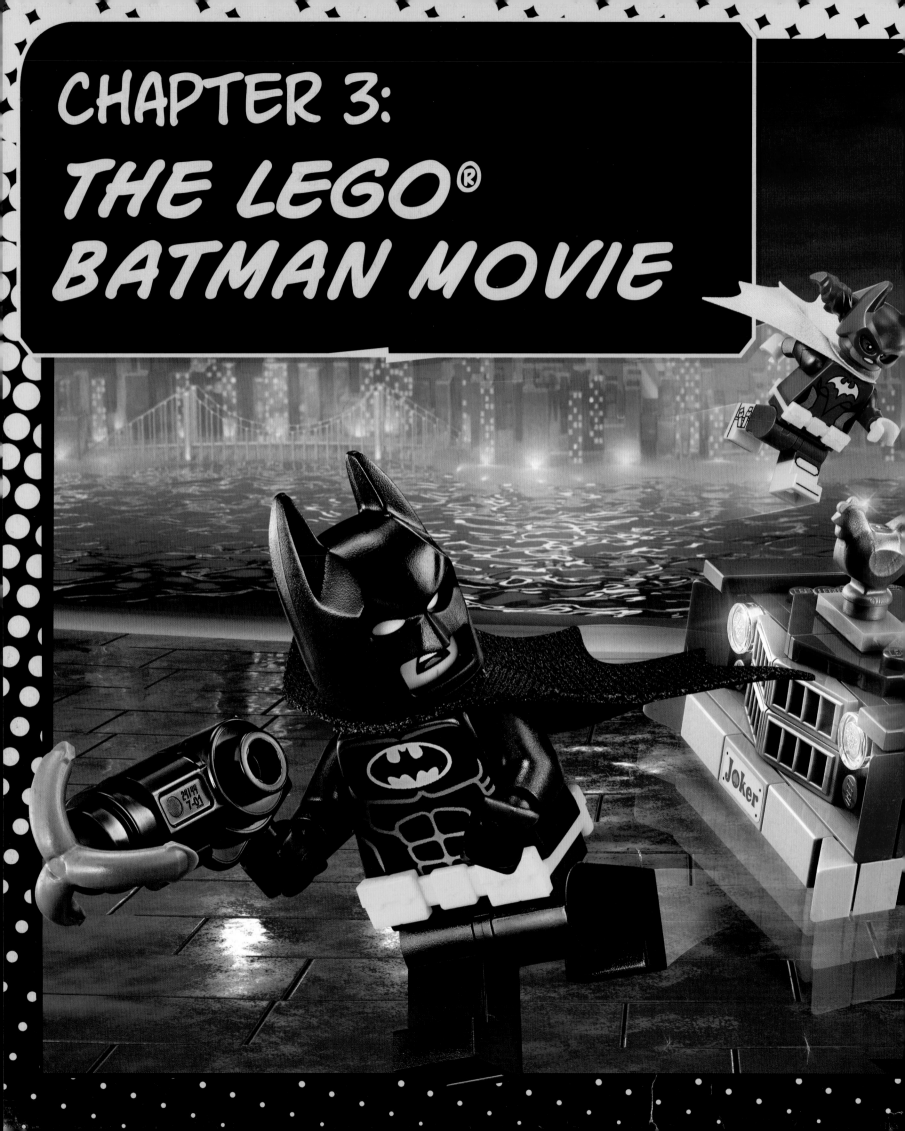

CHAPTER 3:
THE LEGO® BATMAN MOVIE

BATMAN

Batman is back in black for THE LEGO® BATMAN MOVIE. He's a night-stalking, crime-fighting hero, who loves his life and himself. He fights crime alone and doesn't need anyone else. He says he doesn't have any feelings and he doesn't do relationships—but he definitely does cool vehicles. It must be great to be Batman!

Utility Belt also comes in orange and purple

▲ MOVIE BATMAN

Until 2017, Batman's Utility Belt was always printed onto his minifigure. With the movie sets, he gets a molded belt attached to a piece that fits between his torso and legs.

Bow tie

Gold bat-symbol looks like a bow tie

Shiny gold inside to the cape

BRUCE WAYNE

Underneath Batman's cowl is the well-known Bruce Wayne: billionaire, businessman, and Gotham City's most eligible bachelor. Bruce loves parties and attending fancy events.

DISCO BATMAN

Being a Super Hero is a difficult business. Sometimes you need to kick back, put on a sparkly gold cape, and dance and sing all that stress away. Disco Batman is ready to hit the dance floor!

▼ BATMOBILE "THE SPEED WAGON"

This heavy-duty Batmobile is built in the heat of battle, so it looks different from any Batmobile seen before. It can be tricky to park such a big machine in the city, so it has a parallel parking function that turns all the wheels sideways at once.

Cockpit fits both Batman and Robin

Poseable boosters with bat wings

Oversized wheels

Poseable limbs to move the wheels into a different position

Set name	The Batmobile	
Year 2017	Number	70905
Pieces 581	Minifigures	5

▼ THE ULTIMATE BATMOBILE

Batman prefers to work alone, but he comes to realize that sometimes it's good to have friends to help. This mega-build is not just a Batmobile—it's four vehicles in one that can be separated out so members of the Bat-Family have their own craft to help him save the day.

The Batwing sits on top with its wings folded down

The Bat-Tank forms the bulk of the vehicle's rear

The large wheels belong to the Batmobile

Set name	The Ultimate Batmobile	
Year 2017	**Number** 70917	
Pieces 1456	**Minifigures** 8	

Bat-shaped tail wings

BATWING

When the big vehicle breaks up, Batgirl flies the Batwing. It's armed with eight weapons, including two red spring-loaded missiles fired from the back of the craft.

Behind the cockpit is a storage area for weapons or passengers

Rapid-fire six-stud shooter

Wheels are in bike mode

THE BATMOBILE

Full of moving parts, and weapons, this Batmobile is a smaller, compact version of the larger movie one in set 70905, but it makes a great vehicle in its own right.

BAT-TANK

A sturdy, heavy tank with fierce firepower, the Bat-Tank is driven by Alfred wearing an exclusive Batsuit with a bat-chauffeur's cap and a pocket watch on a chain.

BATCYCLE

Robin gets the choice of two vehicles. The motorcycle's chunky double wheels separate and the whole frame rotates so it becomes a hovercraft.

BAT ATTACK

The Wicked Witch of the West, her flying monkeys, and Polka-Dot Man are making mischief in Gotham City. The Bat-Signal flashes in the sky, and Batman and his friends arrive in the Ultimate Batmobile. This amazing auto splits into three more vehicles—Bat-Tank, Batwing, and Batcycle—to chase the villains out of town!

WICKED WITCH OF THE WEST

Broomstick

Spring-loaded shooters

Six-stud rapid shooters

Opening cockpit with dashboard and gearshift

BAT-TANK

Flying getaway saucer

POLKA-DOT MAN

Projected Bat-Signal

BAT-SIGNAL

FLYING MONKEY

Internal LEGO light brick

BATWING

ROBIN

BATCYCLE

Batman fits inside opening cockpit

BATMOBILE

Set name The Ultimate Batmobile	
Year 2017	**Number** 70917
Pieces 1456	**Minifigures** 8

BAT-VEHICLES

In THE LEGO BATMAN MOVIE, Batman has a whole fleet of new vehicles. They're built by Batman on the spot when he needs them, so they have a new style of their own. It's handy being able to create vehicles as he needs them. It means Batman can respond to danger fast with the best vehicle for the job!

Batarang

Set name
Bane Toxic Truck
Attack

Year 2017

Number 70914

Pieces 366

Minifigures 3

▲ THE WHIRLY-BAT FLYER

Batman zooms to the defense of Gotham City in this little Batcopter called the Whirly-Bat Flyer. It's just the thing for when you need to build something and whirl into action.

Net

Bat ears swivel

Net launcher rotates 360 degrees

Push the black button to fire a net over a minifigure

► THE SCUTTLER

Ever seen a crawling, scuttling bat with its wings folded up? Thrown together at Commissioner Gordon's retirement party, the Scuttler is a very unusual batlike vehicle. It can stand on two or four legs, walk, crawl, climb up walls, leap over buildings, and fly away.

Legs can walk on tiptoe or on the larger foot pads

Feet and legs articulate

Beam slides down to lengthen the front legs

Set name The Scuttler

Year 2017   **Number** 70908

Pieces 775   **Minifigures** 6

Flick-fire missile

Set name
Two-Face Double
Demolition

Year 2017

Number 70915

Pieces 564

Minifigures 4

Brick reads "Bat Hawk"

◄ THE BAT HAWK

The Bat Hawk is a low-slung, heavy-duty motorcycle that Batman uses against Two-Face. One side is armed with two stud shooters that can be angled to get the perfect aim. The other side has a single flick-fire missile.

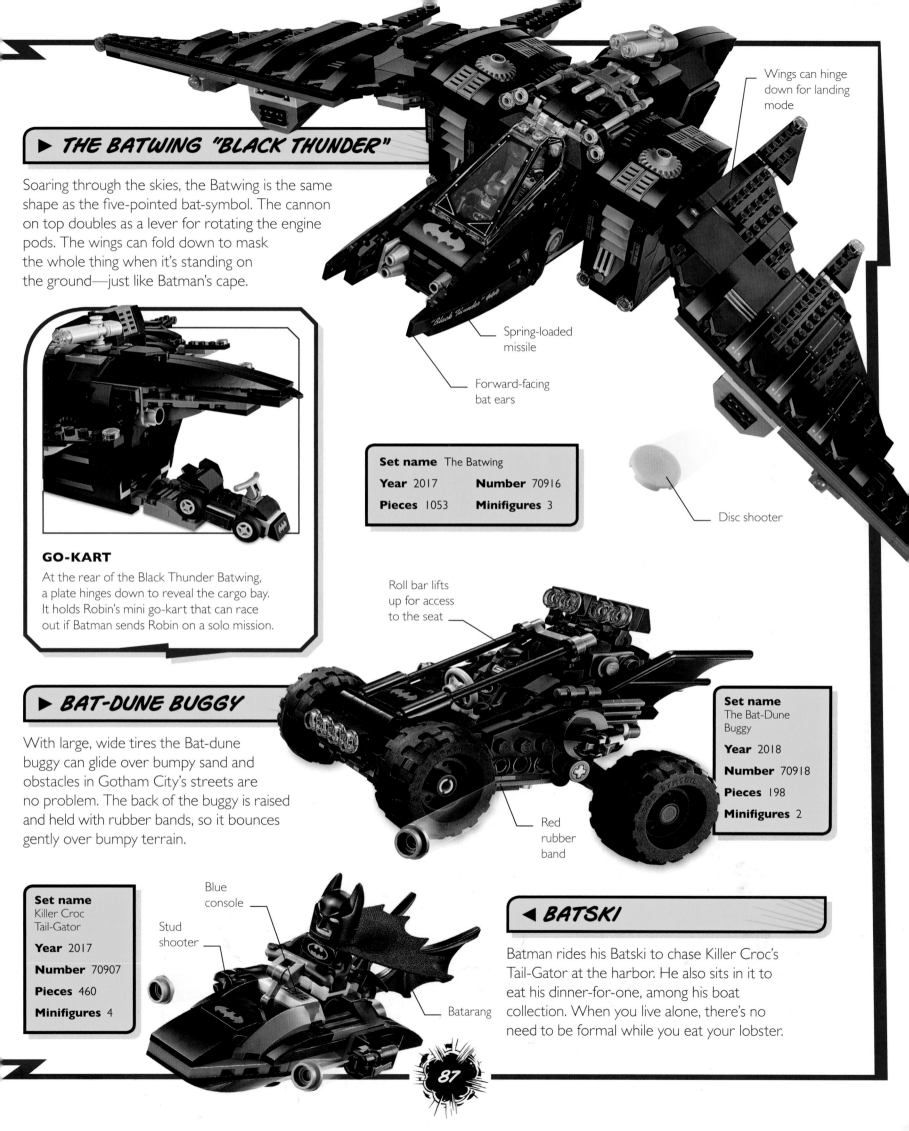

► THE BATWING "BLACK THUNDER"

Soaring through the skies, the Batwing is the same shape as the five-pointed bat-symbol. The cannon on top doubles as a lever for rotating the engine pods. The wings can fold down to mask the whole thing when it's standing on the ground—just like Batman's cape.

Wings can hinge down for landing mode

Spring-loaded missile

Forward-facing bat ears

Disc shooter

Set name	The Batwing	
Year 2017	**Number**	70916
Pieces 1053	**Minifigures**	3

GO-KART

At the rear of the Black Thunder Batwing, a plate hinges down to reveal the cargo bay. It holds Robin's mini go-kart that can race out if Batman sends Robin on a solo mission.

Roll bar lifts up for access to the seat

► BAT-DUNE BUGGY

With large, wide tires the Bat-dune buggy can glide over bumpy sand and obstacles in Gotham City's streets are no problem. The back of the buggy is raised and held with rubber bands, so it bounces gently over bumpy terrain.

Set name	
The Bat-Dune Buggy	
Year 2018	
Number 70918	
Pieces 198	
Minifigures 2	

Red rubber band

Blue console

Stud shooter

Set name	
Killer Croc Tail-Gator	
Year 2017	
Number 70907	
Pieces 460	
Minifigures 4	

Batarang

◄ BATSKI

Batman rides his Batski to chase Killer Croc's Tail-Gator at the harbor. He also sits in it to eat his dinner-for-one, among his boat collection. When you live alone, there's no need to be formal while you eat your lobster.

BAT-SPACE SHUTTLE

Crime stretches far beyond Gotham City—even out into space! Batman is prepared with a spaceship for tackling intergalactic villains. His shuttle separates easily into four parts. The largest part is a fuel tank, and the two black rocket boosters help the shuttle power off. They separate after takeoff, leaving the shuttle to fly into space.

IN CONTROL

Like most of Batman's vehicles, there is space for only one hero pilot in this space shuttle. The cockpit opens up and has a command seat for the pilot and a control panel that the pilot uses to fly the shuttle.

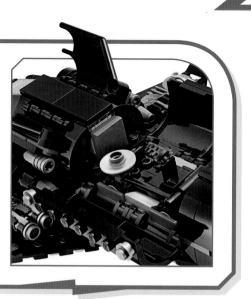

Set name	
The Bat-Space Shuttle	
Year 2018	
Number 70923	
Pieces 643	
Minifigures 6	

TAKEOFF

Takeoff requires plenty of fuel and power! Once in space, with the press of a lever, the large, gray fuel tank and boosters detach from the shuttle.

▶ DOCKING PAD

The Bat-Space Shuttle set can attach to the Batcave Break-In set (pp.90–91). The docking pad has a preparation area, launchpad, costume rail, moon buggy, and a Bat-kayak. The weapons rack is stocked with a stud shooter, Batarangs, a grappling hook, and three sturdy arrows.

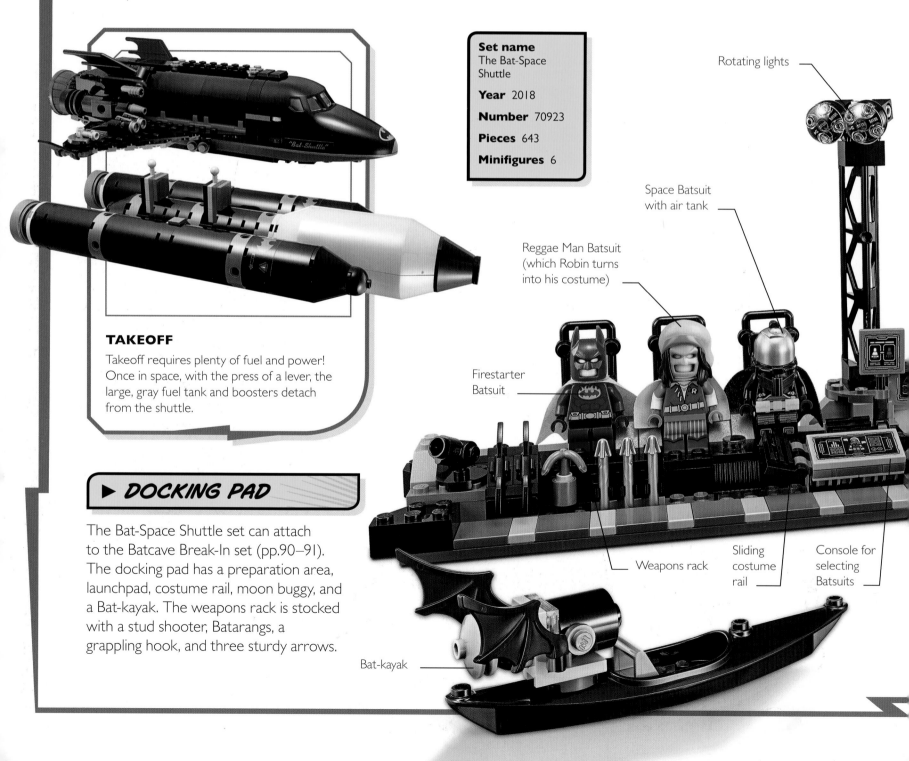

Rotating lights

Space Batsuit with air tank

Reggae Man Batsuit (which Robin turns into his costume)

Firestarter Batsuit

Weapons rack

Sliding costume rail

Console for selecting Batsuits

Bat-kayak

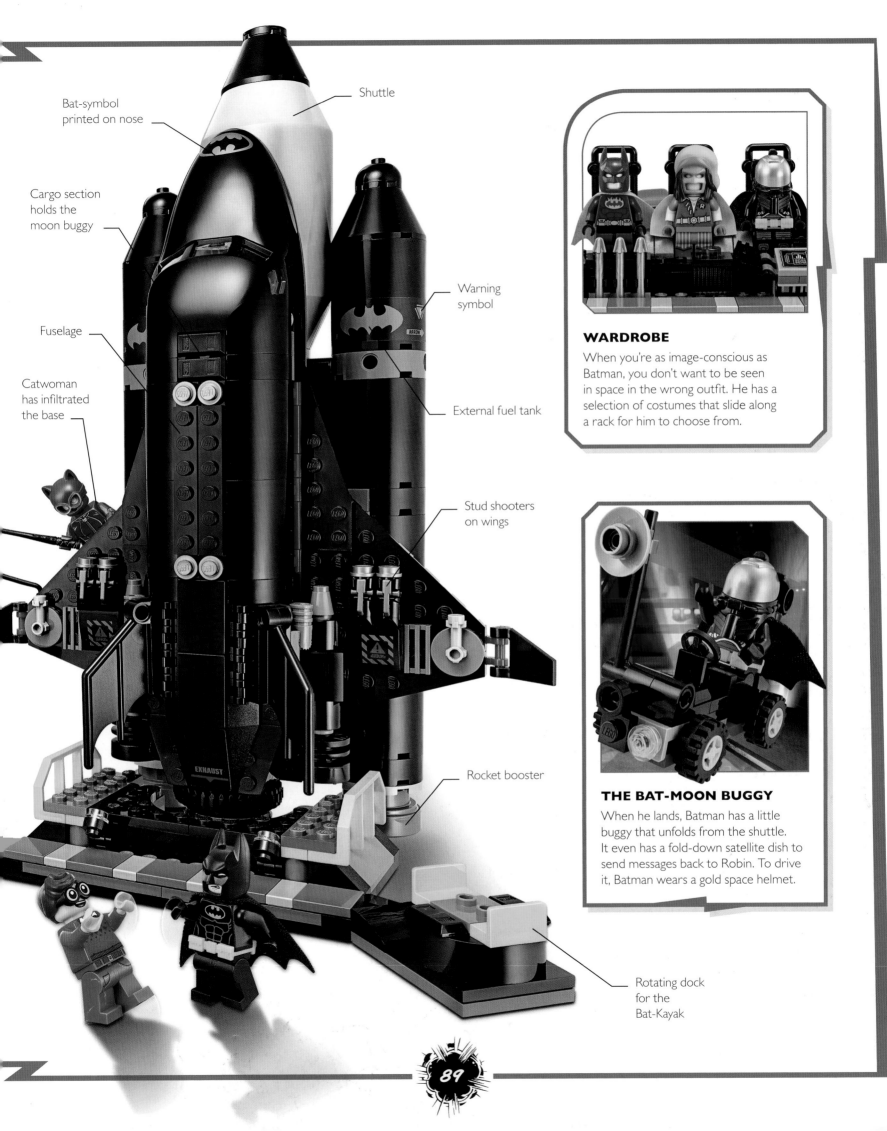

Bat-symbol
printed on nose

Shuttle

Cargo section
holds the
moon buggy

Fuselage

Catwoman
has infiltrated
the base

Warning
symbol

External fuel tank

Stud shooters
on wings

Rocket booster

EXHAUST

WARDROBE

When you're as image-conscious as
Batman, you don't want to be seen
in space in the wrong outfit. He has a
selection of costumes that slide along
a rack for him to choose from.

THE BAT-MOON BUGGY

When he lands, Batman has a little
buggy that unfolds from the shuttle.
It even has a fold-down satellite dish to
send messages back to Robin. To drive
it, Batman wears a gold space helmet.

Rotating dock
for the
Bat-Kayak

THE BATCAVE

Deep below Wayne Manor, on Wayne Island, is Batman's secret headquarters. Does Batman live in Bruce Wayne's basement, or does Bruce Wayne live in Batman's attic? Whichever it is, he needs to watch out for the Penguin who wants to invade the Batcave in his Duckmobile.

COMMAND CENTER

At the heart of the Batcave is the command center. From here, Batman can surveil every corner of his cave. In case of surprise intruders, there are Batarangs behind the consoles!

► SECRET LAIR

Batman's secret headquarters includes a rotating wardrobe and a changing room. A moving platform acts as an elevator, moving minifigures from one floor to another, and a "Batwalk" platform runs across the full length of the cave.

Button for opening back of the cell to allow for break-ins and escapes

Bat-pack Batsuit

Scu-Batsuit

Raging Batsuit for boxing

A vertical hangar rotates Batman's outfits. Each is a complete minifigure, with a white head

Moving platform transports outfits or minifigures up to the office or upper level

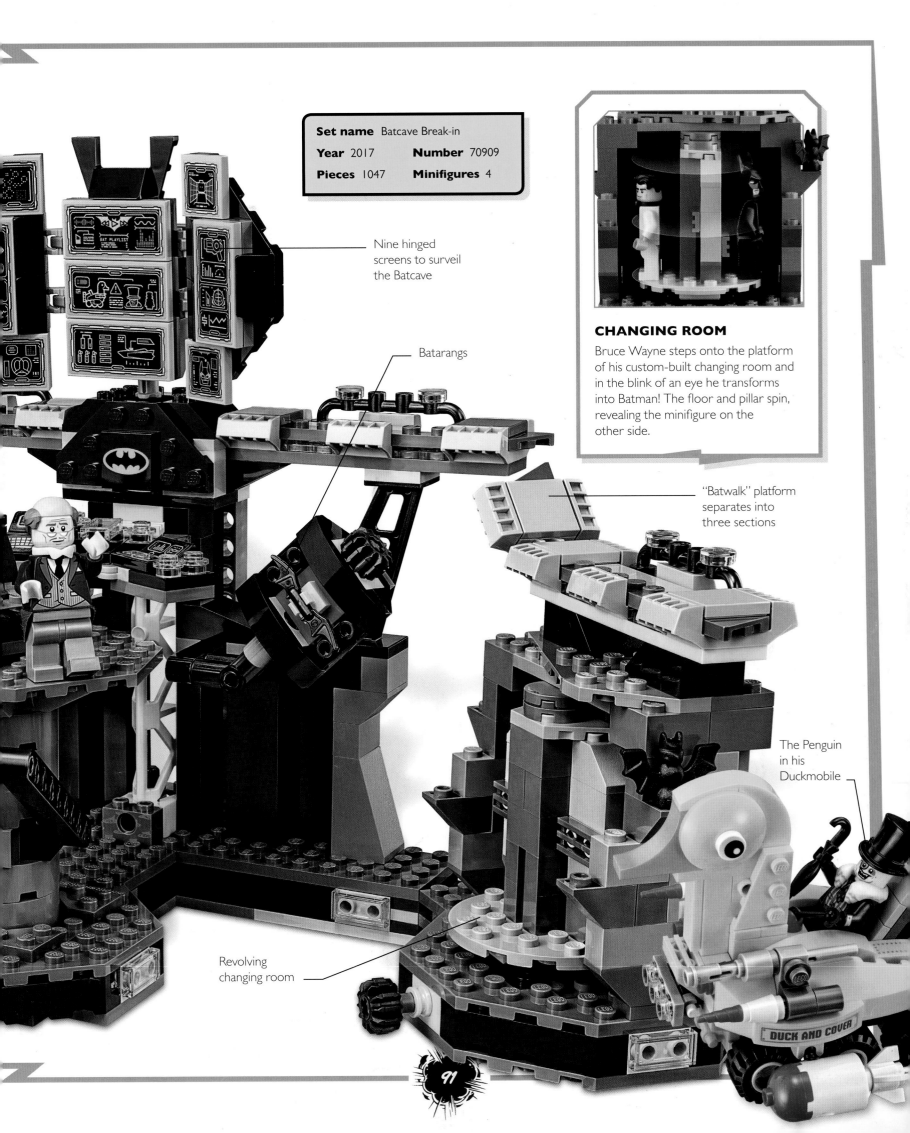

Set name	Batcave Break-in	
Year 2017		**Number** 70909
Pieces 1047		**Minifigures** 4

Nine hinged screens to surveil the Batcave

Batarangs

CHANGING ROOM

Bruce Wayne steps onto the platform of his custom-built changing room and in the blink of an eye he transforms into Batman! The floor and pillar spin, revealing the minifigure on the other side.

"Batwalk" platform separates into three sections

The Penguin in his Duckmobile

Revolving changing room

DUCK AND COVER

MOVIE MATES

Batman works alone. Always has. Always will. He protects other people—and himself—by pushing them away. But one day, it turns out that it takes a team, not just a Batman, and that Batman actually stands for "Best at Teamwork" Man. Here is one big happy fraternity of people who do an awesome job together.

Pinstripe vest

Police badge

▲ BARBARA GORDON

Welcome to the new commissioner. . . Barbara Gordon. Top of her class at Harvard for Police, she cleaned up the streets of Gotham City's nearby sister city Blüdhaven using statistics and compassion. And now she's bringing her new ideas and her nunchucks to Gotham City.

NIGHTWING

In his new minifigure based on THE LEGO BATMAN MOVIE, Nightwing is wearing his underwear outside his pants for the first time. He doesn't look very pleased about it.

Clip-on bat wings

Cowl is wonky

Extra-long cape

▼ DICK GRAYSON

Orphan Dick Grayson is wide-eyed to meet his hero Bruce Wayne. His red sweater and blue pants are based on his outfit in the 1960s TV series, but he hasn't aged a day.

Very big eyes

DISCO ROBIN

How do you celebrate saving the city? You don a shiny white and gold ensemble and hit the disco, of course.

Reggae Man's pants were a little tight, so Robin ripped them

Ruffled shirt

TUXEDO

Dressed to impress. Dick's looking for a home and a family. What could be better than Bruce Wayne as your dad? Except maybe Batman as your second dad, too.

▲ ROBIN

Nimble, small, and quiet when he wants to be, Robin is exactly who Batman needs to infiltrate the Fortress of Solitude. He gets a special costume adapted from Batman's Reggae Man outfit.

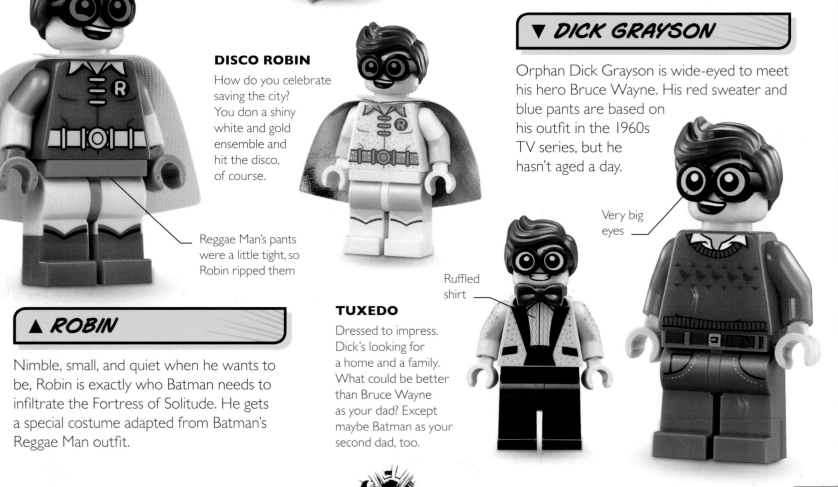

▼ BATGIRL

Barbara takes a leaf out of Batman's book and turns caped crusader, pairing purple with yellow instead of black. She's Batman's platonic coworker buddy, who's a girl, but just a friend. And she kicks everyone's butt and uses her head to save Gotham City.

Ponytail can clip off cowl

Cape is white on the other side

Metallic finish on the inside of the cape

DISCO BATGIRL
Fighting crime is a serious business, but Batgirl isn't afraid to let her hair down, then tie it back up in a white disco cowl, and start dancing.

Yellow Batarang

BAT BUTLER
Alfred takes his role as Batman's father figure seriously, even dressing the part in his own Batsuit.

Coattails

▲ ALFRED PENNYWORTH

Batman's British butler likes everything spick and span. He keeps everything in order, from life in the Batcave and Batman's diary to his own appearance. He looks super smart in his morning coat, wing collar, and pinstripe vest.

▶ JAMES GORDON

After years of police service, Jim Gordon looks as pleased as punch at his retirement party. His proud face and shiny medals celebrate his record as commissioner of Gotham City. He can relax knowing his city's now in his daughter's capable minifigure hands.

Sharp white gloves

Ceremonial sash

Police badge on arms

▶ MAYOR MCCASKILL

A vote for Mayor McCaskill is a vote for protecting Gotham City with help from the police, but mostly from pressing the Bat-Signal to call on Batman. And that's the way he likes it. Madam Mayor means business with her solid hairstyle and blue power suit.

String of pearls

THE JUSTICE LEAGUE

It's party time in Superman's Fortress of Solitude! Members of the Justice League are celebrating the group's 57th anniversary party—but Batman didn't get an invitation. To really get the party started, turn the lever behind the DJ booth to make the revolving dance floor spin!

Set name	
The Justice League Anniversary Party	
Year 2018	Number 70919
Pieces 267	Minifigures 4

Nervous smile

◀ SUPERMAN

The host of the party, Superman is in his bright-blue suit with red trunks. This minifigure has two expressions: one side is full of the joys of partying, but the other looks embarrassed for when Batman turns up unexpectedly!

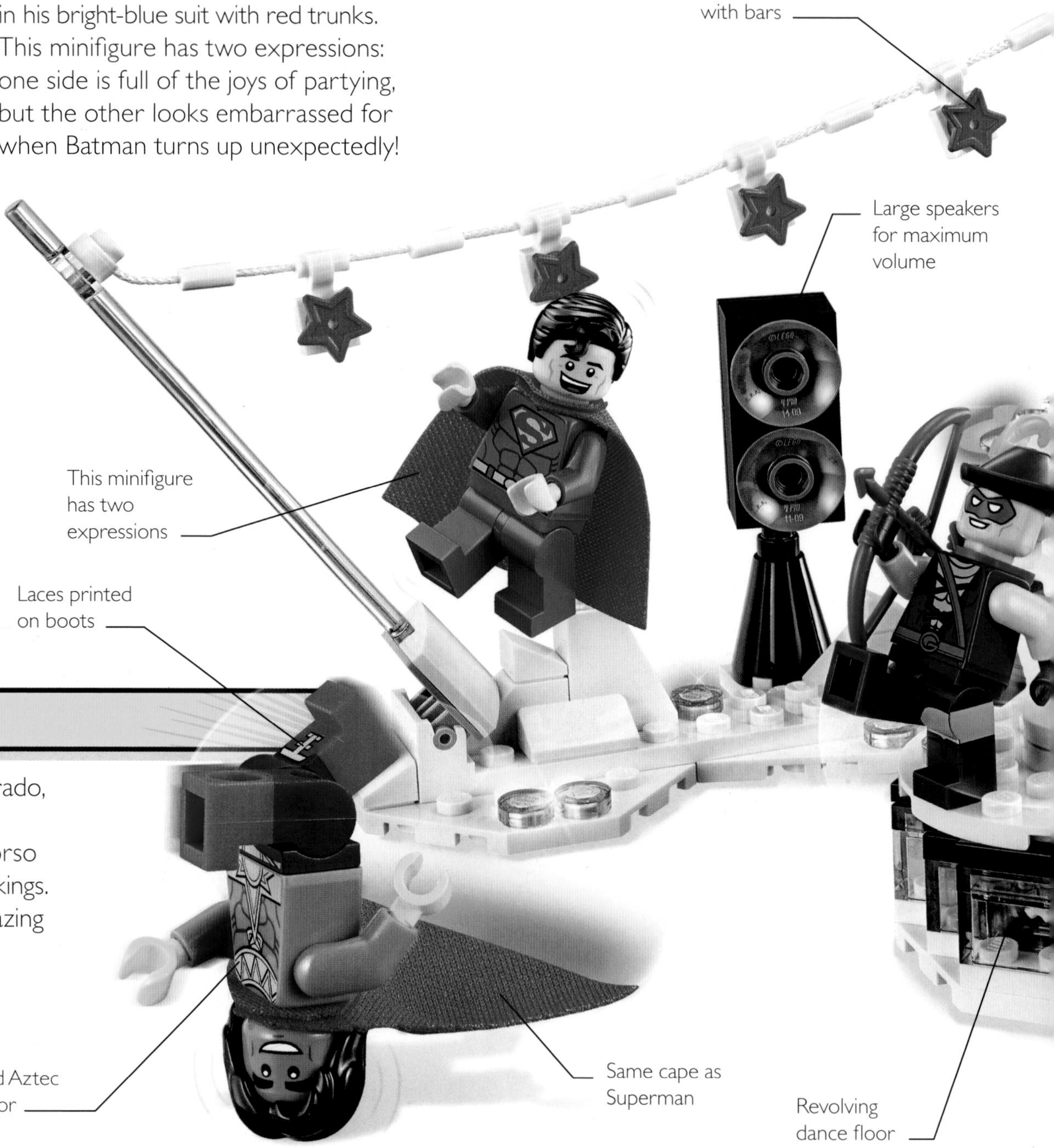

Arms and legs twist on the dance floor

This minifigure has two expressions

Laces printed on boots

Party decorations hang on a LEGO string with bars

Large speakers for maximum volume

▶ EL DORADO

The Mexican Super Hero, El Dorado, is dressed to party in his brightly colored costume. His detailed torso printing is inspired by the Aztec kings. He is enjoying showing off his amazing dance moves!

Gold Aztec armor

Same cape as Superman

Revolving dance floor

▶ GREEN ARROW

That's not a party mask—it's the Green Arrow! This minifigure has swapped his compound bow for a classic one, plus a quiver of arrows on his back. His feathered party hat is inspired by his childhood hero, Robin Hood.

▼ WONDER DOG

If you want to request a song from the DJ, you need to speak to Wonder Dog. He's got his front paws up on the decks for mixing the disco tunes. The blue dog from the Super Friends team is molded from a single LEGO piece with face printing, and he wears a soft, green cape.

White fur on his nose

57th Annual
JUSTICE LEAGUE
Anniversary Party

Records have a bat-symbol print

DJ decks

Dual face with smile or a grimace expression

Outstretched wings

Disco lights

▲ HAWKGIRL

Superpowered by a belt made from Nth Metal, Hawkgirl is in the Super Friends team as well as the Justice League. Her minifigure comes with two sets of detachable wings: one folded up and the other outstretched for really letting loose on the dance floor.

BANE

Huge Bane is one of Batman's most physically strong and most intelligent enemies, but he has a weakness. He is dependent on a substance called Venom for his superpowers. Without it, he will never defeat Batman. He breathes Venom through a mask and, in a pack on his back, keeps a supply plugged into his body via tubes.

Large sheepskin collar

Big black boots

◄ BANE BIG FIGURE

Bane has appeared as five minifigures, but his THE LEGO BATMAN MOVIE version is a "big figure"—a larger scale figure, as befits his bulging muscles. A stud on each upper arm connects flex hoses that deliver Venom from his backpack, which also attaches to his body with studs.

Big figure fits standing on the truck to operate the shooter

Six-stud rapid shooter

Set name	Bane Toxic Truck Attack	
Year 2017		Number 70914
Pieces 366		Minifigures 2

► BANE'S TOXIC TRUCK

Bane's Monster-style truck can be tilted back on its four rear wheels to increase the field of fire from the shooter. The back wheels also have suspension, which means that the truck travels well over bumpy ground. Bane uses the vehicle to attack Gotham City with barrels of toxic waste.

Detachable toxic tank

Side rails fold down

TWO-FACE

A character of two halves, Two-Face's THE LEGO BATMAN MOVIE minifigure reflects his dual nature. He has been a master of crime—and Batman's enemy—ever since half of his face was badly injured in an attack. Once a criminal lawyer, he's now gone over to the wrong side of the law—even his "good side" is a nattily dressed crime boss.

Blue scarf for a sharp crime lord

▶ SPLIT PERSONALITY

On one half of his body, Two-Face looks respectable in a three-piece suit—except for the fierce, growling expression on his face. On the other half, acid has eaten away much of his face, skin, and clothes, leaving dripping pink hair… and revealing a surprising glimpse of heart-covered underwear!

▲ JAILBIRD

While imprisoned in Arkham Asylum in THE LEGO BATMAN MOVIE, Two-Face's split style is mostly covered up by an orange prison jumpsuit. Only his face and hands show his true nature.

Tinted purple window pane

This scoop bucket is unique to this set

NO ORDINARY TRUCK

The "regular" side of the truck claims to belong to "Falcone's Legit Construction Company" according to the sticker on the side. It could almost be an ordinary LEGO build.

No corresponding lights on this half

Blades on the wheels do extra damage

Set name	
Two-Face Double Demolition	
Year	2017
Number	70915
Pieces	564
Minifigures	4

▲ TWO-FACE EXCAVATOR

Just like Two-Face's face and body, this truck is two different halves put together into one whole. It's an articulated front loader designed to do as much damage as possible with its hefty bulk, an excavator arm for scooping or ram-raiding, and wheel spikes.

TOXIC ATTACK

Batman pilots his Whirly-Bat at breakneck speed, looking to strike a vital blow with a Batarang as Bane, powered up with Venom, fires toxic missiles from his Toxic Truck! Can the Dark Knight stop Bane and his Mutant Leader ally from turning Gotham City into a toxic dump?

Rotating rotor blades

Spare Batarang

Adjustable Batwing

Toxic bomb about to explode

BATMAN

WHIRLY-BAT

Dangerous chemicals warning logo

ACE CHEMICALS

Toxic waste spill

TOXIC WASTE SILO

Six-stud rapid shooter

Target-sighting element

Bane big figure with poseable arms and legs

Backpack with Venom tubes

TOXIC TRUCK

Mutant Leader in cockpit

BANE

Detachable toxic tank

Big wheel

Rear four-wheel suspension

Set name	Bane Toxic Truck Attack	
Year 2018		**Number** 70914
Pieces 366		**Minifigures** 2 plus big fig

Driving goggles

Cat-shaped zipper

Utility Belt piece

CATWOMAN

Cunning Catwoman is most often seen in black, but in THE LEGO BATMAN MOVIE, she got a purple makeover, including a molded Utility Belt, like Batman's. Batman's whip-cracking feline foe is still the Princess of Plunder. She is an expert at helping herself to sparkling, priceless jewels—and making a super-fast getaway in her Catcycle.

► ARKHAM INMATE

Locked up in Arkham Asylum, Catwoman's 2017 movie minifigure keeps her head and purple gloves, but now she wears an orange prison jumpsuit like all the other inmates. Her Utility Belt is bursting with equipment so she won't be stuck in there for long!

Prison jumpsuit

▲ PURPLE CATSUIT

Appearing in Catwoman Catcycle Chase and The Bat-Space Shuttle sets, Catwoman has an all-new purple catsuit. Her cowl has driving goggles built in over her large green eyes, and she wields her favorite whip to make sure any enemies keep their distance!

Stolen ruby

Adjustable handlebars

Purple headlight

Wide tires for good grip on streets of Gotham City

◄ THE CATCYCLE

Stop, thief! Catwoman rides her black and purple Catcycle to the jewelry store for a gemstone raid and then speeds away from the scene of the crime. Robin and Batgirl will have a hard time catching her!

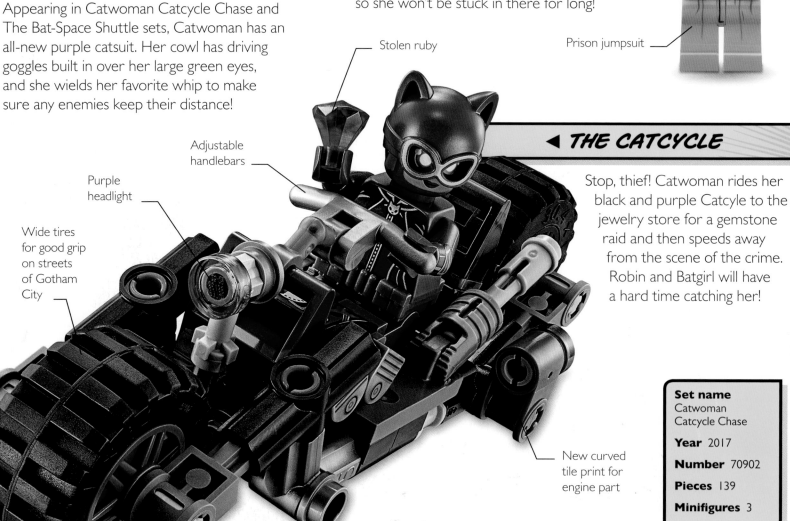

New curved tile print for engine part

Set name
Catwoman
Catcycle Chase

Year 2017

Number 70902

Pieces 139

Minifigures 3

THE PENGUIN

He may look like a gentleman, but there's nothing gentle about the Penguin. This villain is one of Gotham City's fishiest gangsters. In THE LEGO BATMAN MOVIE, he's up to his old tricks, bothering Batman and even busting into the Batcave. What's more, this time he has new hench-penguins to help him!

Trademark top hat

Monocle

Fancy fur collar

▼ THE DUCKMOBILE

It's brightly colored and looks like a cute rubber duck, but it's armed with missiles! The Duckmobile can sail through water and drive over land. It's just what the Penguin needs for an attack on Wayne Island.

HENCH-PENGUIN

Beware the Penguin's little, red-eyed, robot penguin helpers. They can wear harnesses with tools and weapons to cause maximum damage.

Set name
Batcave Break-in
Year 2017
Number 70909
Pieces 1047
Minifigures 7

Propeller

Lights can be angled

Sticker says "Duck and Cover"

▲ DAPPER PENGUIN

For THE LEGO BATMAN MOVIE the Penguin sports a new natty top hat and a unique fluffy collar piece. His suit jacket is open, revealing a striped vest that is straining over his bulging belly.

▼ THE ARCTIC ROLLER

The Penguin drives a long-nosed, classic-style car with runner boards. Push the button on the hood of the elegant car to fire two spring-loaded missiles.

Hood ornament looks like a penguin head

Removable roof

Fish missiles

Set name
The Penguin Arctic Roller
Year 2017
Number 70911
Pieces 305
Minifigures 2

Informal look with no suit jacket

New detailed stripes

Club and heart printing

Skull-shaped buttons

THE JOKER

He always comes to work with a smile, but there's nothing funny about the Joker. He's Batman's greatest enemy —or at least he likes to think so. He believes that what he and Batman have is special and that they need each other as foes in order to have purpose.

Clear transparent neck bracket

Long coattails

▲ MOVIE JOKER

For THE LEGO BATMAN MOVIE, the Joker's outfit has a new design. His face wears a fanged smile on one side and a clownlike grin on the other. He also has new arm printings. One arm has a club and heart and the other has a diamond and a spade.

DISCO JOKER

When the Batcave is turned into the Joker Manor, the Joker has a snazzy disco suit with a gold "J" medallion, shutter shades, and long white coattails.

MODEL PRISONER

The Joker gives himself in to the Gotham City police and is soon wearing an orange Arkham Asylum jumpsuit. However, it's all part of his devious plan.

BALLOON ESCAPE

The Joker is up, up, and away with his detachable balloon backpack. He floats into the air, leaving Batman to deal with the large bomb he's planted at the Gotham City Energy Facility.

▼ THE NOTORIOUS LOWRIDER

Bouncing through the Gotham City streets on its elaborate suspension, the Joker's car is hard to miss with its striking purple and green livery. If Batman gives chase, the Joker simply opens the trunk and fires two spring-loaded missiles at him. Blue LEGO® Technic pins behind the driver's seat operate the weapons.

Spare tire on trunk, which opens

Chicken hood decoration

Exhaust heads

Clown horn

Body of car lifts up on each wheel

Set name	
The Joker Notorious Lowrider	
Year 2017	**Number** 70906
Pieces 433	**Minifigures** 3

THE RIDDLER

In THE LEGO BATMAN MOVIE, Batman's puzzle-obsessed foe joins the Joker. The Joker's plan is for all villains, including all those in the Phantom Zone prison dimension, to team up to destroy Gotham City—which, it turns out, is flimsy and built over an eternal abyss. They'd better get to work. After all, the city won't blow *itself* up!

Question mark

Purple mask

Hair is attached to the hat piece

▶ QUIZZICAL INMATE

In Arkham Asylum, the Riddler has to wear a prison jumpsuit. His orange outfit is the same as the other inmates, except for his green, gloved hands. He wears his new hat on his double-sided head, which smirks on one side and frowns on the other.

▼ RIDDLE RACER

The Riddler races around Gotham City in his nifty green and white sports car. In The Riddle Racer, he uses it to battle Batman, teaming up with Kite Man, Magpie, and Calendar Man. In his Riddle Racer, he can charge up behind unsuspecting heroes, lift the two flaps on the front of the vehicle, and fire the two spring-loaded shooters hidden inside. A secret front compartment conceals two guns.

Set name	The Riddler Riddle Racer	
Year 2017		**Number** 70903
Pieces 254		**Minifigures** 5

Tilted bowler hat

Cheeky grin

Rear cover is usually a windshield piece

Wing mirror

Question mark logo

Body is very low to the ground

Hinged panel hides guns

BIG-SCREEN RIDDLER

While he's free from the law, the Riddler struts his stuff in a sharp new green suit, with a jacket covered in tiny question marks. His cane sports a new question mark piece.

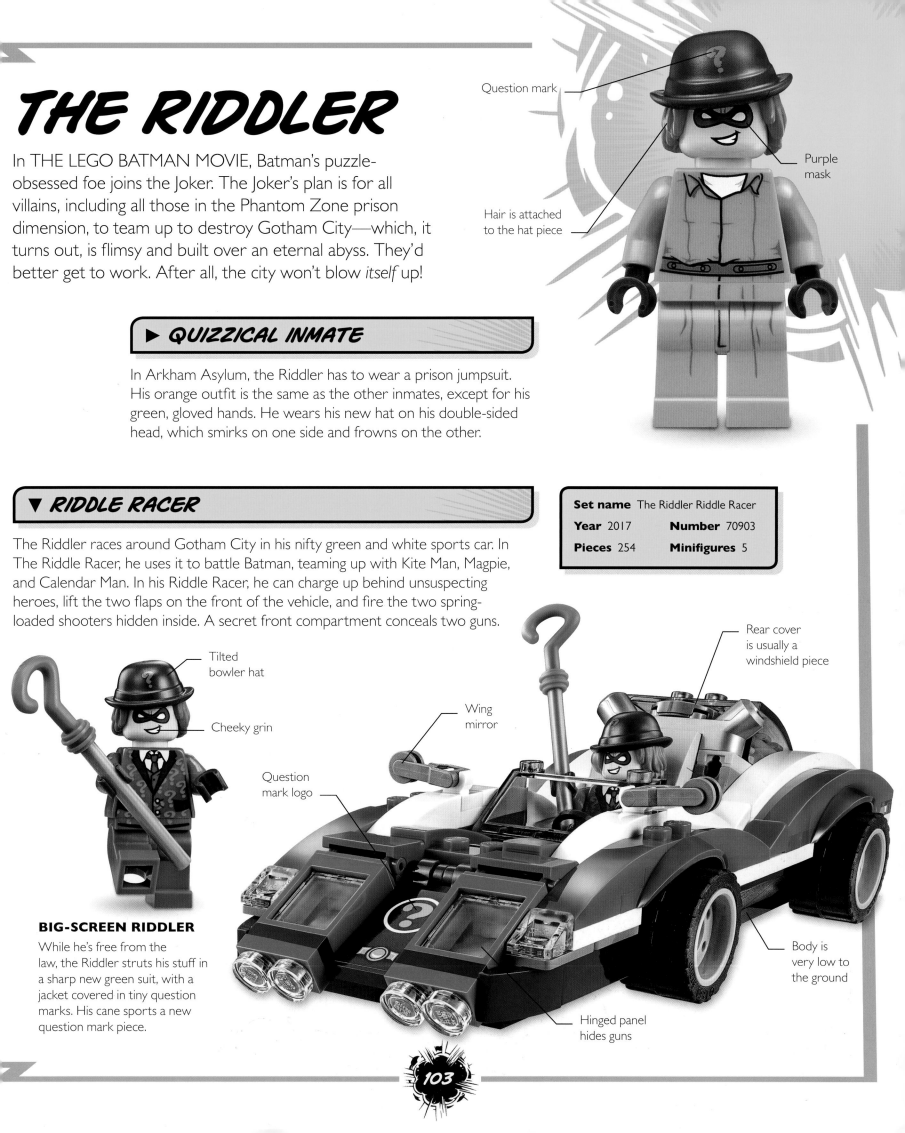

THE JOKER MANOR

The Joker has "Jokerized" Wayne Manor! Batman, Batgirl, Alfred, and Nightwing have joined forces to reclaim the grand estate from the Clown Prince of Crime. The heroes have to try to make their way through Joker Manor and avoid all of its traps and pitfalls.

The Joker's hilarious makeover of Wayne Manor is anything but subtle. A roller coaster encircles the mansion. A huge Joker head has been erected over the rear entrance, with a slide emerging from the mouth. The Manor is protected by a rotating "big eye" tower, which is on the alert for intruders!

MANIC MUSIC STUDIO

Batman's in the mansion's music studio. The studio features a mixing desk made of LEGO tiles and a swivel chair. Is he using the microphone and loudspeakers to contact his friends for help?

Set name	The Joker Manor	
Year 2017	**Number** 70922	
Pieces 3444	**Minifigures** 10	

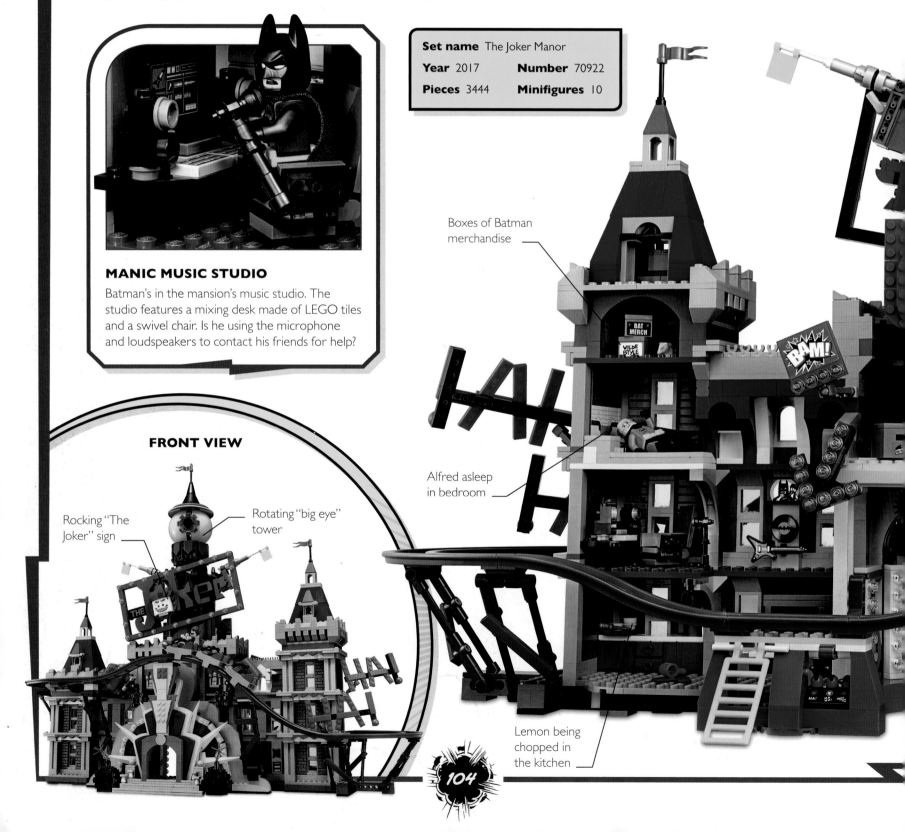

Boxes of Batman merchandise

Alfred asleep in bedroom

FRONT VIEW

Rocking "The Joker" sign

Rotating "big eye" tower

Lemon being chopped in the kitchen

REDECORATING

This Joker minifigure has tattoo printing on his arms and a dapper suit. He replaces Batman's family portraits with posters of himself made of stickered LEGO tiles. This makes him so happy, he has a gruesome grin!

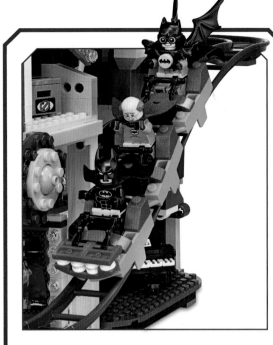

CRIME COASTER

Batman, Alfred, and Nightwing escape to the roller coaster. The three lime green roller coaster cars may look rickety, but they have side guards to keep them on the track.

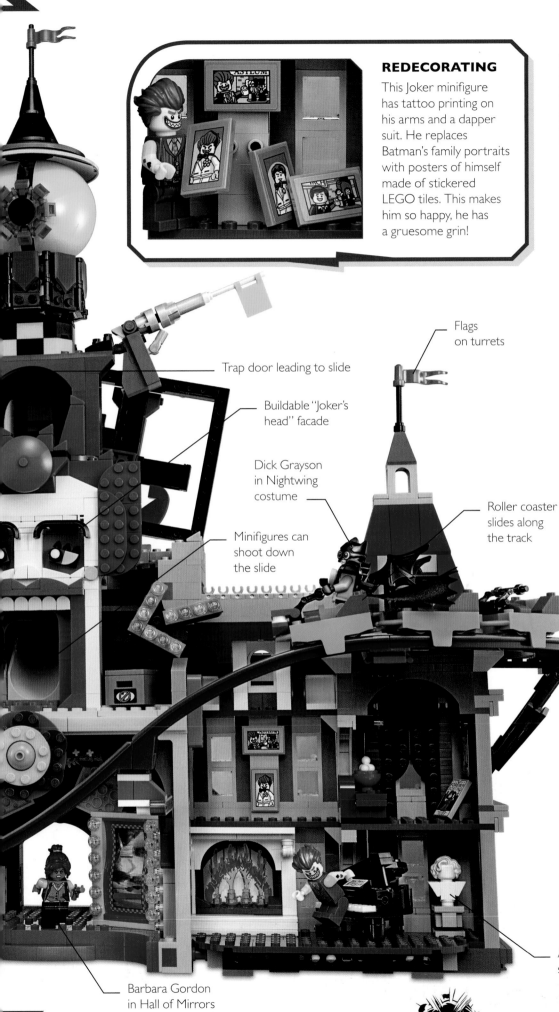

Flags on turrets

Trap door leading to slide

Buildable "Joker's head" facade

Dick Grayson in Nightwing costume

Minifigures can shoot down the slide

Roller coaster slides along the track

Barbara Gordon in Hall of Mirrors

Antique statue

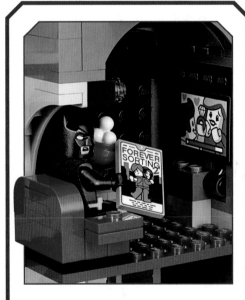

CAPED CRUSADER CINEMA

After battling the Joker, Batman unwinds in his cinema room which has a cozy chair, large movie screen and a bowl of popcorn. The DVD case for the movie "Forever Sorting 2" is a printed tile.

Red and black pigtails

Kneepads

HARLEY QUINN

Dr. Harleen Quinzel was once a psychologist at Arkham Asylum. Then her life became extraordinary when she decided to go off on a series of adventures alongside Arkham's most notorious bad boy, the Joker! Now the terrible twosome causes chaos all over Gotham City!

Baseball bat decorated with diamond motifs

▲ MOVIE QUEEN HARLEY

This Harley Quinn minifigure is based on 2017's THE LEGO BATMAN MOVIE. She's printed with incredible detail from head to toe, like the "playing-card diamond" beauty mark on her cheek, the bow tie around her neck, and the roller derby–style kneepads on her legs. She's Harley Quinn, movie queen!

SKATER HARLEY

Harley Quinn is careening through Gotham City on her roller skates! Dynamic printing on her torso and arms shows off her new jacket. She always keeps her trusty baseball bat close at hand!

DR. HARLEEN QUINZEL

This is what Harley looked like when she was Harleen Quinzel, dressed in a lab coat and Argyle sweater. She looks cheerful, but her double-sided head reveals a puzzled stare.

ID card printed on legs

WEAPON

Harley's oversized, circus-themed mallet has "bull's-eye" designs on either side. Harley's signature "diamond" emblem trails around the cylindrical hammerhead. Don't touch it or Harley will get upset!

Cape features "skull" emblems

SURE SHOT

Not everyone would enjoy being shot out of a cannon, but Harley seems to be loving it! She certainly looks the part in her fancy red, white, and black outfit.

◄ HARLEY'S TRUCK

Harley's truck features an elevating and rotating cannon with a transparent "flame" element. The driver's cabin doors open, and the hood reveals engine elements. One press of a big, red button fires Harley out of the cannon!

MALLET

Set name
Harley Quinn
Cannonball Attack

Year 2018

Number 70921

Pieces 425

Minifigures 4

Rear tires

Opening hood

THE SCARECROW

Jonathan Crane was a doctor who was obsessed with the science of fear. Disguised as the ghoulish Scarecrow, he sets out to frighten everyone in Gotham City. His special fear gas brings people's worst nightmares to life, making him one of Batman's most formidable foes.

Hat is bent at top

Patches printed on jacket

▶ GRIM GYRO

The Scarecrow's Gyro-Copter takes to the sky, spreading fear and panic! This horrifying helicopter features top and rear spinning rotors and an adjustable rudder. Two green fear gas bombs drop from this creepy contraption. Can Batman foil the spooky Scarecrow's gas attack?

Spinning rotors

Halloween pumpkin logo

Set name	
Scarecrow Fearful Face-Off	
Year 2017	**Number** 70913
Pieces 141	**Minifigures** 2

Witch's broom runner

▲ SCREEN SCARE

This Scarecrow minifigure from 2017 is based on his appearance in THE LEGO BATMAN MOVIE. Red eyes peer out through his creepy mask. A battered hat and patched, tattered clothes complete his wild, vagabond look.

◀ PIZZA PANIC

The Scarecrow typically turns an everyday sight into a fearful event when he makes a special pizza delivery. Instead of mouth-watering pizza, the Scarecrow's cart contains a cargo of a very different kind—homemade, "deep panic" fear gas!

Rotate sign to release fear gas canister

Flame pattern on helmet

DEVIOUS DELIVERY BOY

The Scarecrow poses as a pizza delivery boy in a motorcycle helmet and printed T-shirt.

Set name	Scarecrow Special Delivery
Year 2017	**Number** 70910
Pieces 204	**Minifigures** 3

Printed scales

KILLER CROC

A bizarre skin condition made Waylon Jones an outcast until, as Killer Croc, he got a job wrestling alligators in a sideshow carnival. Ferocious and super strong, he turned to crime and now relishes every battle with Batman!

◄ BRUTE FORCE

THE LEGO BATMAN MOVIE Killer Croc is a big figure, to emphasize his physical power. He has a poseable head with snapping jaws and posable arms and wrists. No chain can hold Croc—check out the broken ones hanging from his wrists!

Clawed hand with gripping fingers

Eight-ball stick shift

Broken chain

Tarantula

Cow skull ornament

► TAIL-GATOR

Killer Croc's Tail-Gator looks roughly cobbled together, but it's a super-charged, big-wheeled, intimidating vehicle. The turn of a knob deploys one crate filled with frogs and another filled with dynamite! While his allies can ride in the cabin, the steering column and printed eight-ball gearshift are designed for Croc alone.

Zebra Man

Wooden plank

Set name		
Killer Croc Tail-Gator		
Year 2017	**Number** 70907	
Pieces 460	**Minifigures** 3	

MR. FREEZE

Ever since a lab accident permanently lowered his body temperature, Dr. Victor Fries has to wear a special suit to keep himself permanently chilled. Searching for a cure for his condition, and turning to a life of crime in order to fund scientific research, Victor calls himself Mr. Freeze.

Face blue with cold

Ice seeping out of suit

Transparent element

▶ COOL CUSTOMER

THE LEGO BATMAN MOVIE minifigure has intricately delineated eyepieces and dials on his protective suit, as well as kneepads and silver metal toecaps. The armor piece he wears over his head and shoulders is removable!

WEAPON

Mr. Freeze's most famous weapon is his freeze gun, which generates a fast-freezing gas that can trap victims in a solid block of ice! The gun is topped off with a stud shooter. The weapon can be held by Mr. Freeze or by his Exosuit mech.

FREEZE GUN

Hoses carry freezing chemicals

Red eyepieces

ICE PRISON

An unfortunate security guard becomes encased in a block of ice while trying to stop Mr. Freeze! This transparent blue ice structure is hinged, so it's easy to trap a minifigure inside and just as easy to free them!

▶ MR. FREEZE MECH

Mr. Freeze is even more intimidating in his Exosuit mech, which allows him to tower over Batman! The mech's backpack unit locks the cool criminal firmly in place. Transparent hoses reveal the blue-tinged chemicals that keep Mr. Freeze supercool as he aims his favorite freeze gun at a fresh target.

Set name
Mr. Freeze Ice Attack

Year 2017

Number 70901

Pieces 201

Minifigures 3

Poseable leg

Ball-and-socket joint

109

ARKHAM ASYLUM

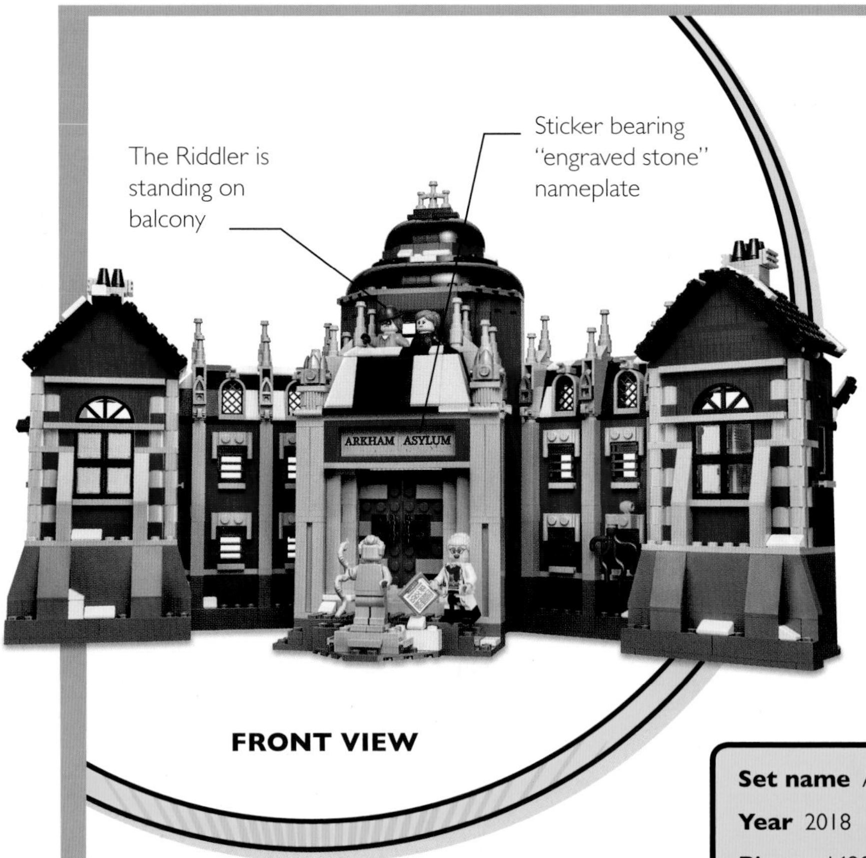

The Riddler is standing on balcony

Sticker bearing "engraved stone" nameplate

ARKHAM ASYLUM

FRONT VIEW

If you've tussled with Batman, you've probably bunked at Arkham at least once! The inmates most famously detained at this lousy lockup include the Joker, Poison Ivy, Two-Face, Catwoman, and Scarecrow. The Asylum is covered in snow. Batman must banish the Joker and his super-villain friends using his Phantom Zone Projector element to help him.

Set name	Arkham Asylum	
Year 2018	Number	70912
Pieces 1628	Minifigures	12

Computer monitor in guard tower

Walkie-talkie

Poison Ivy idles by guardrails

LOCK DOWN

VISITATION AREA

Arkham's visitation area features a removable "glass" partition with phones on each side. Dr. Harleen Quinzel is talking to the Joker. Security cameras watch their every move.

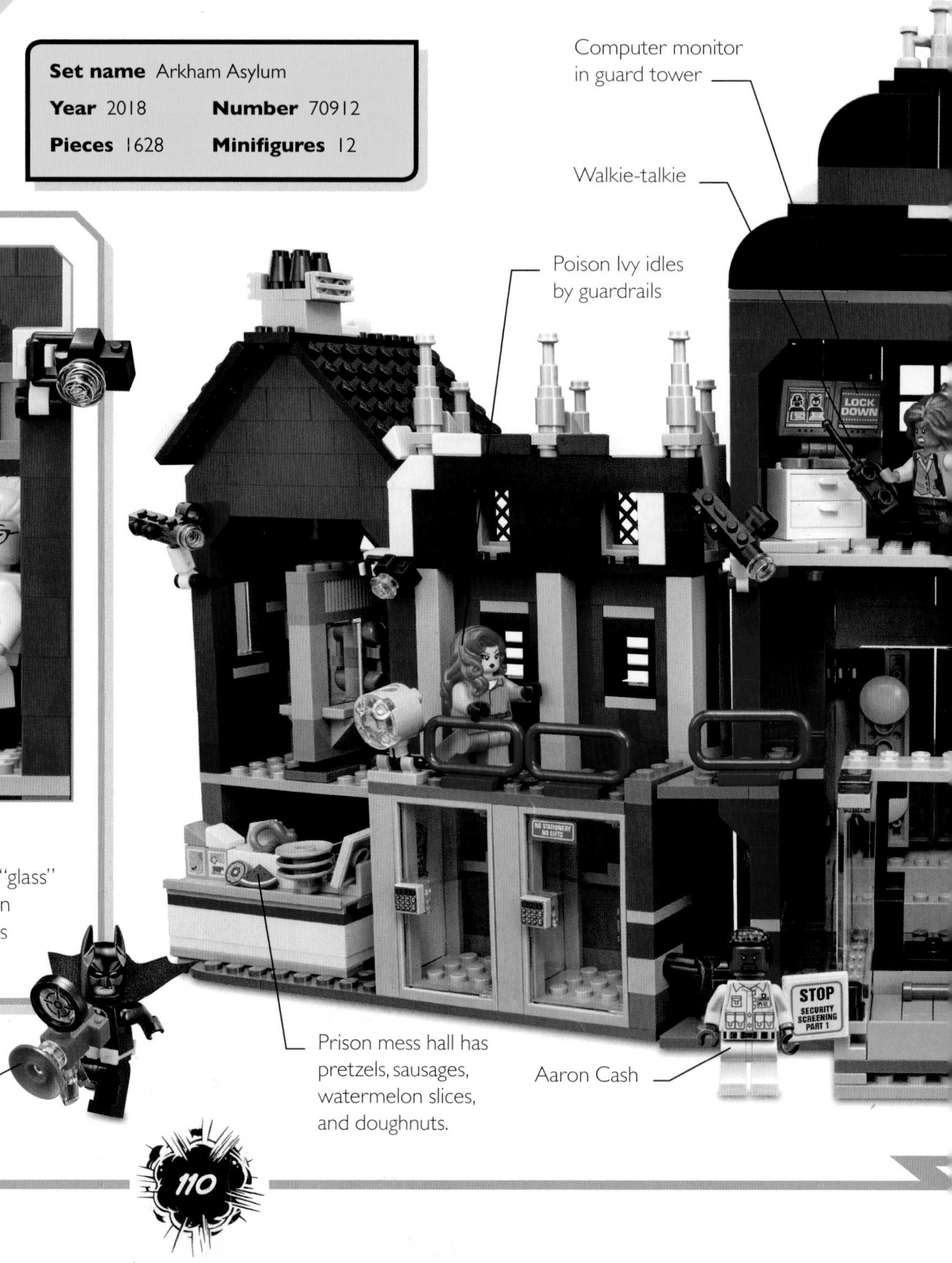

Phantom Zone Projector

Prison mess hall has pretzels, sausages, watermelon slices, and doughnuts.

Aaron Cash

STOP SECURITY SCREENING PART 1

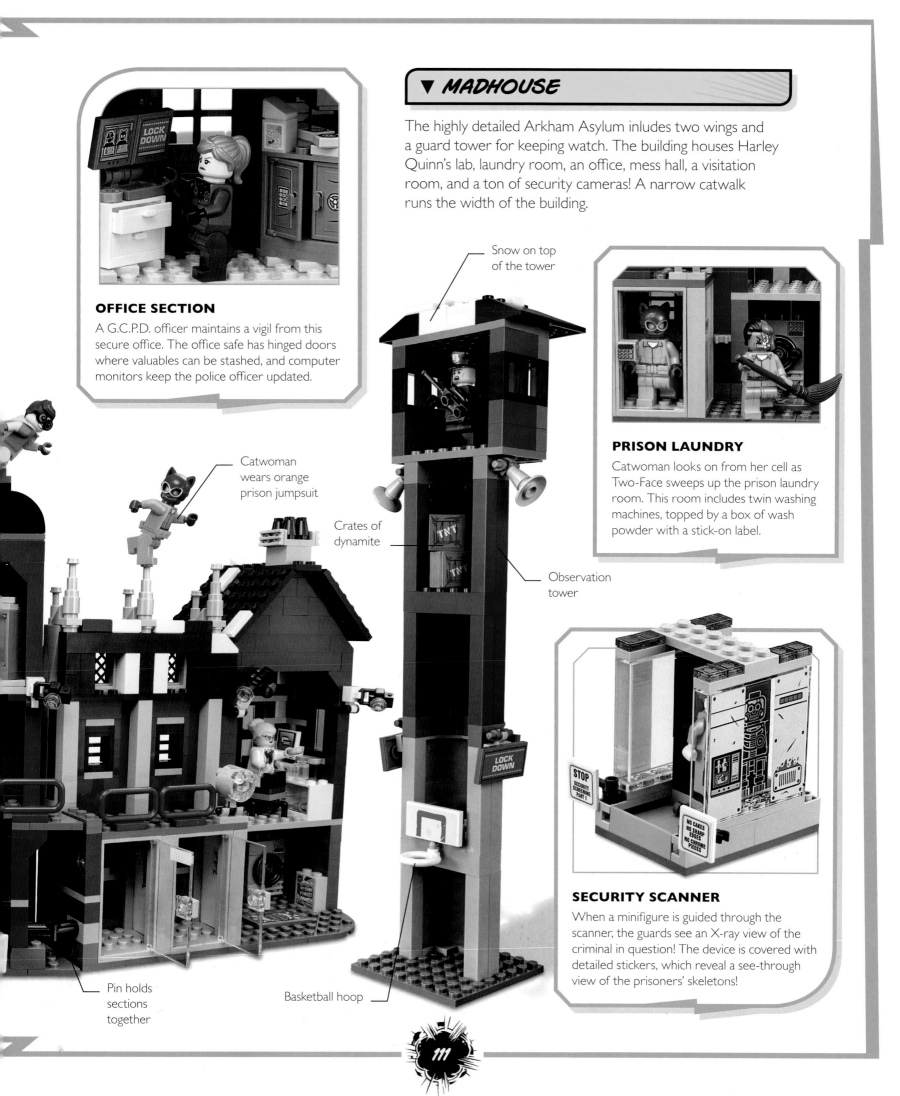

The highly detailed Arkham Asylum inludes two wings and a guard tower for keeping watch. The building houses Harley Quinn's lab, laundry room, an office, mess hall, a visitation room, and a ton of security cameras! A narrow catwalk runs the width of the building.

OFFICE SECTION

A G.C.P.D. officer maintains a vigil from this secure office. The office safe has hinged doors where valuables can be stashed, and computer monitors keep the police officer updated.

Snow on top of the tower

Catwoman wears orange prison jumpsuit

Crates of dynamite

Observation tower

Pin holds sections together

Basketball hoop

PRISON LAUNDRY

Catwoman looks on from her cell as Two-Face sweeps up the prison laundry room. This room includes twin washing machines, topped by a box of wash powder with a stick-on label.

SECURITY SCANNER

When a minifigure is guided through the scanner, the guards see an X-ray view of the criminal in question! The device is covered with detailed stickers, which reveal a see-through view of the prisoners' skeletons!

WEIRD ROGUES

Batman's enemies come in all shapes and sizes, and they hail from all over the world. Two of them even come from the magical land of Oz! Here's the lowdown on some of the weirdest and wackiest Batman foes, as they appear in the THE LEGO BATMAN MOVIE.

Kite Man's body and helmet are printed with kite symbols, matching his super-villain name. His red glider wings are hinged so that they can be angled in flight. He needs to hope for a windy day to have a chance of beating the Batman!

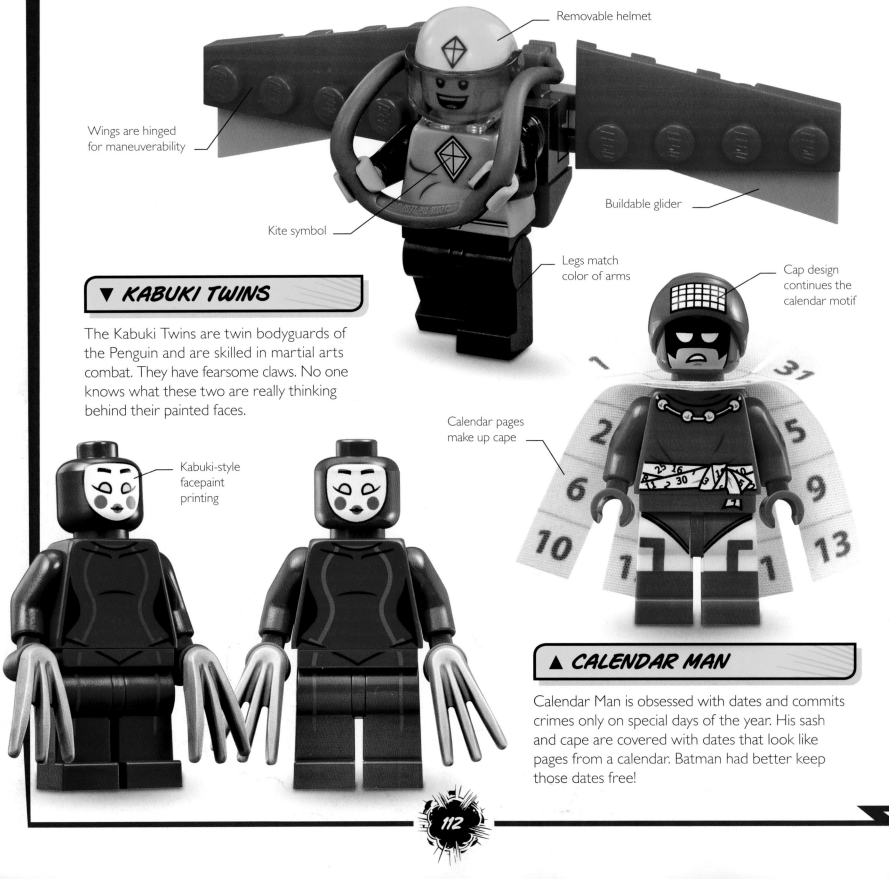

Removable helmet

Wings are hinged for maneuverability

Buildable glider

Kite symbol

Legs match color of arms

Cap design continues the calendar motif

▼ KABUKI TWINS

The Kabuki Twins are twin bodyguards of the Penguin and are skilled in martial arts combat. They have fearsome claws. No one knows what these two are really thinking behind their painted faces.

Kabuki-style facepaint printing

Calendar pages make up cape

▲ CALENDAR MAN

Calendar Man is obsessed with dates and commits crimes only on special days of the year. His sash and cape are covered with dates that look like pages from a calendar. Batman had better keep those dates free!

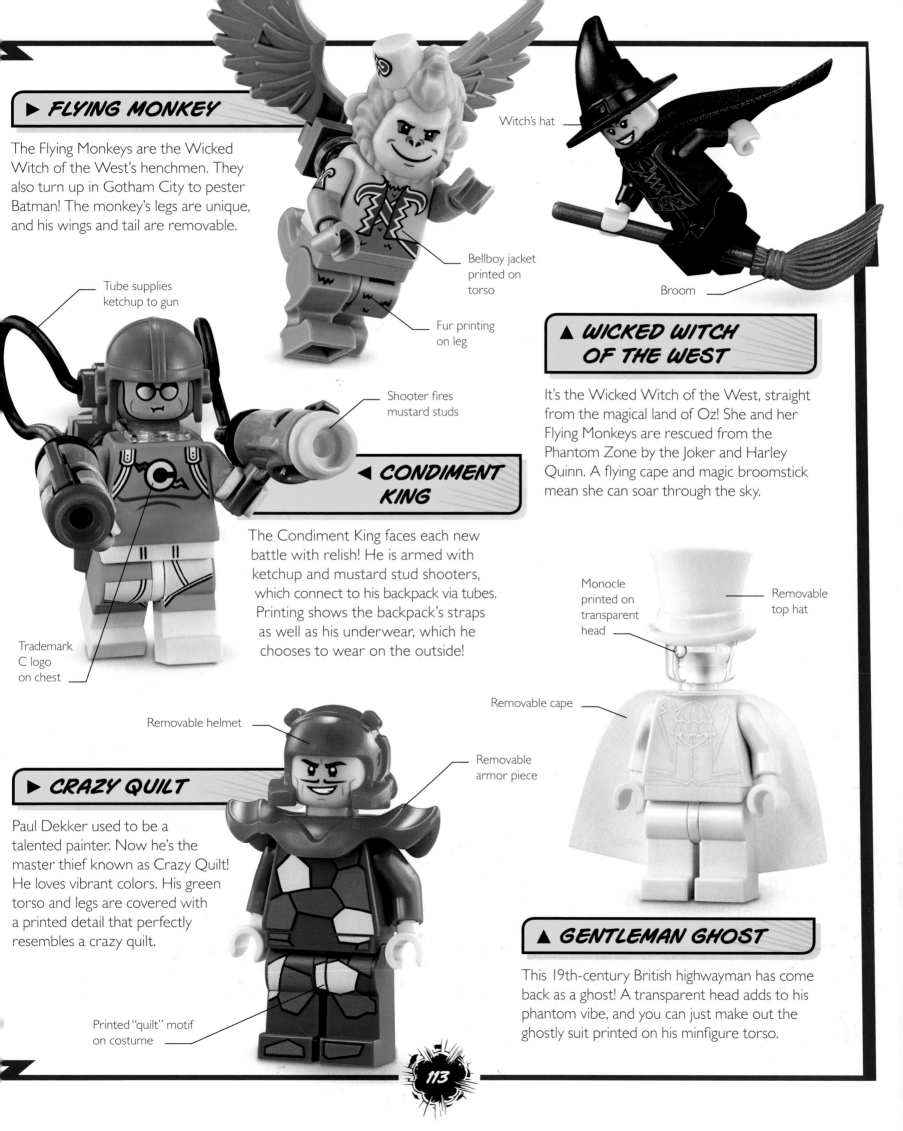

► FLYING MONKEY

The Flying Monkeys are the Wicked Witch of the West's henchmen. They also turn up in Gotham City to pester Batman! The monkey's legs are unique, and his wings and tail are removable.

Bellboy jacket printed on torso

Fur printing on leg

Tube supplies ketchup to gun

Shooter fires mustard studs

◄ CONDIMENT KING

The Condiment King faces each new battle with relish! He is armed with ketchup and mustard stud shooters, which connect to his backpack via tubes. Printing shows the backpack's straps as well as his underwear, which he chooses to wear on the outside!

Trademark C logo on chest

Witch's hat

Broom

▲ WICKED WITCH OF THE WEST

It's the Wicked Witch of the West, straight from the magical land of Oz! She and her Flying Monkeys are rescued from the Phantom Zone by the Joker and Harley Quinn. A flying cape and magic broomstick mean she can soar through the sky.

Monocle printed on transparent head

Removable top hat

Removable cape

Removable helmet

Removable armor piece

► CRAZY QUILT

Paul Dekker used to be a talented painter. Now he's the master thief known as Crazy Quilt! He loves vibrant colors. His green torso and legs are covered with a printed detail that perfectly resembles a crazy quilt.

Printed "quilt" motif on costume

▲ GENTLEMAN GHOST

This 19th-century British highwayman has come back as a ghost! A transparent head adds to his phantom vibe, and you can just make out the ghostly suit printed on his minifigure torso.

CRAZY CROOKS

Batman has his hands full with this kooky collection of criminals from THE LEGO BATMAN MOVIE. Some are colorful, some are a bit creepy, some are sensational, and some are just plain scary! They employ super-science, poisonous plants, traps, tricks, and weapons to defeat the Dark Knight—but they fail every time!

Domino mask

Tarantula emblem

Sai knife

▲ TARANTULA

Former FBI agent Catalina Flores is the Tarantula! She is highly skilled in hand-to-hand combat and is armed with two silver sai weapons. If those things don't put off her enemies, her fierce glare definitely will!

▼ POISON IVY

Smart scientist Poison Ivy has all sorts of plant-based powers. Her torso printing features a leafy dress and vine necklace. Watch out—those vines she's holding are highly poisonous!

Elaborate curls

Vines used as weapons

Mohawk hair piece mimics a zebra's stiff mane

Stripe printing

◄ ZEBRA MAN

Thanks to an accident, scientist Jacob Baker found himself with magnetic waves imprinted, zebra stripe-style, all over his body. With his incredible magnetic powers, he can attract or repel virtually any object at will!

Stripes continue on torso

Removable armor piece

Dress printed on legs

Flower

Prison jumpsuit

ARKHAM ASYLUM IVY

Here, Poison Ivy is dressed in a prison jumpsuit. Even though she's in jail, she still has green fingers!

▲ MAGPIE

Super sneaky thief Magpie adores bright, sparkly jewels. She is a talented thief and when she steals something shiny, she leaves an explosive booby trap in its place!

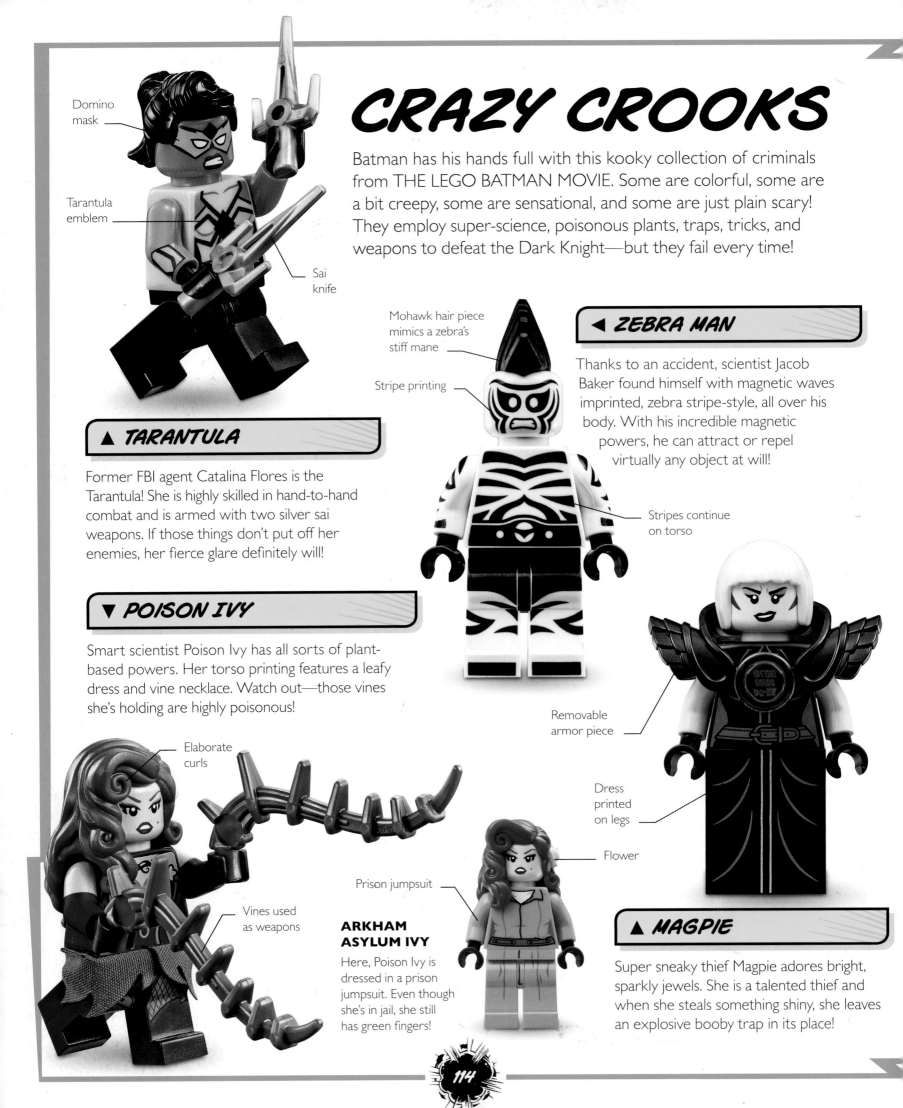

► CLAYFACE

Clayface is a shape-changing blob. This brick-built figure has poseable arms, legs, and a head, as well as three interchangeable hands: two stud shooters and one clay hammer!

Yellow eyes

Clay hammer hand

Stud shooter hand

Helmet with polka dot printing

◄ POLKA-DOT MAN

As Polka-Dot Man, Abner Krill commits polka-dot-themed crimes. This minifigure is drenched in printed dots. Even his goggle lenses are dots. He's not always this happy: rotate his head to reveal his frightened face!

► CAPTAIN BOOMERANG

There's no mistaking Captain Boomerang—he has boomerang designs all over his costume and has a couple of real ones ready to throw. No matter how hard Batman tries to defeat him, this villain always returns.

Boomerang accessory

Torch has transparent fire element

Bald dome piece

► EGGHEAD

He thinks he's the world's smartest criminal. Dressed in egg-themed yellow and white, Egghead is capped with a bald dome piece, making his head more egg-shaped. He's carrying a dinosaur egg, which he hopes to hatch out in order to cause trouble for Robin and Batgirl.

Dinosaur egg

Wrist guard is printed on

► MUTANT LEADER

With his teeth filed to sharp points and his fiery torch, Mutant Leader is used to getting his own way. He bosses around the Mutants street gang and is a useful ally to major villains, like Bane.

MOVIE MINIFIGURES

Batman has had a very busy career as a crime fighter. He has donned many different costumes during his adventures! He has also made many quirky friends and enemies. This collection of minifigures appears in the 2017 THE LEGO BATMAN MOVIE!

THE COLLECTIBLE MINIFIGURE CLAN

GLAM METAL BATMAN

Batman is really ready to rock in this costume, which has a silver bat-symbol on the cowl and a bat-symbol on each boot.

Electric guitar

Spiky shoulder pieces

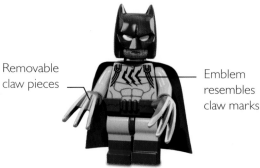

CATMAN

A trapper of big cats who becomes a criminal, Thomas Blake is Catman. The whole world is his scratching post!

Removable claw pieces

Emblem resembles claw marks

Printed tearing at the seams

Leopard-skin pelt

CLAN OF THE CAVE BAT

This club-wielding "prehistoric Batman" features a printed animal skin outfit, stone medallion, and wrist guards.

Rolled-up sleeves

Walkie-talkie

Joker "Wanted" poster

COMMISSIONER GORDON

James Gordon has vowed to clean up Gotham City. He has a shoulder holster, tie clip, and G.C.P.D. badge.

Wand with star-shaped tip

Transparent pink wings

Removable tutu

FAIRY BATMAN

In his ceaseless fight against crime, Batman has mastered every skill, even ballet. Fairy Batman is perfectly primped to pirouette!

Uniquely molded head piece

Flippers for arms

ORCA

Marine biologist Dr. Grace Balin transforms herself into a humanoid orca with powers to match.

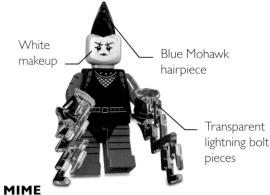

White makeup

Blue Mohawk hairpiece

Transparent lightning bolt pieces

MIME

Mime artist Camilla Ortin has electric gloves to commit crimes. She hates noise, so she zaps her foes as quietly as possible!

Molded cowl is removable

Bathrobe printing

LOBSTER-LOVIN' BATMAN

Batman is ready to relax in the Batcave with a lobster dinner. The lobster piece rests on a plate with lettuce and butter!

Silver Batgirl emblem

Hot pink Batarang

Pharaoh's headdress

Cane with cobra-head design

Real snake

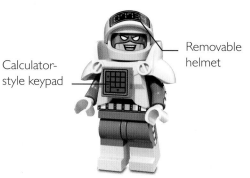

Beaming with pride

Handcuffs

On-off button for Bat-Signal

PINK POWER BATGIRL

When they first team up, Batman shows Barbara Gordon many different costumes she could wear as Batgirl.

KING TUT

William McElroy is a college professor who has turned to crime and thinks he's the ancient Egyptian pharaoh King Tut!

BARBARA GORDON

Barbara Gordon shines in her G.C.P.D. outfit. Its sash continues on her back. Her cap is attached to her hair piece.

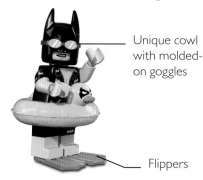

Unique cowl with molded-on goggles

Flippers

Hairpiece covers sad face

Fang poking out of mouth

Removable handcuffs

Removable helmet

Calculator-style keypad

VACATION BATMAN

This is Batman in a fun-loving vacation mood. The floatie ring's duck head even sports a Batman-style mask!

ARKHAM ASYLUM JOKER

The Joker has been nabbed. His Arkham jumpsuit is full of printed detail. Turn his two-sided head to see his sad face.

CALCULATOR

This mathematical malefactor's helmet visor has "07734" printed on it. Turn it upside down, and it reads "hello!"

Head piece resembles a pencil eraser

Notebook is a LEGO tile

Removable nurse's cap

Elaborate detail on shoes

Helmet attaches to collar piece

THE ERASER

Lenny Fiasco is an expert at erasing crime evidence. He has a unique head piece, and his shoes form a pencil point!

NURSE HARLEY QUINN

Nurse Harley Quinn's clipboard has a picture of her boyfriend, the Joker, and "H & J" inside a love heart!

RED HOOD

Take off this mysterious criminal's helmet and you'll see…a face-obscuring mask! A collar piece holds his helmet in place.

Rabbit-ear cowl

Cowl is printed on head

Crab represents zodiac sign of Cancer

Fish represents zodiac sign of Pisces

Glasses attached to hair piece

Robins printed on sweater

MARCH HARRIET

Harriet Pratt is a cottontail criminal. Detail includes a white bow around her collar and wrist guards on her arms.

ZODIAC MASTER

Zodiac symbols are printed all over this master's costume. Even his weapons are based on zodiac signs.

DICK GRAYSON

Dick is Robin's alter ego—and there are robins on his sweater. He may look a little shy, but he's ready for action!

CHAPTER 4:
BEHIND THE SCENES

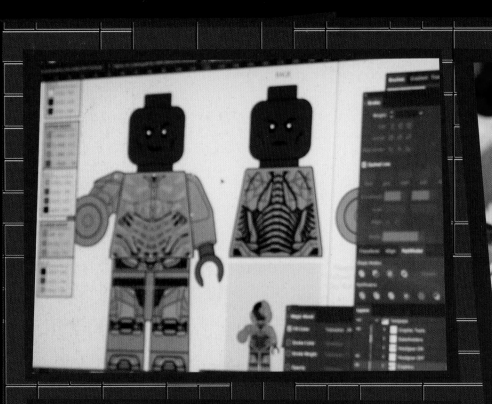

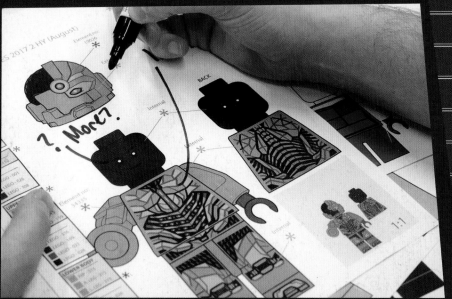

MEET THE TEAM!

The LEGO® DC Super Heroes team works in Billund, Denmark. They are responsible for creating the sets and minifigures for the theme. We asked them some questions to find out more about how your favorite LEGO DC Super Heroes sets were created. Let's meet the team!

"I create toys to make people smile. That is my contribution to the world."

ALICE GEIGER

Clockwise from left:
Alice Kate Millard (Designer), Bjarke Lykke Madsen (Design Master), Mark Tranter (Designer), Casper Glahder (Designer), Christopher Terrance Peron (Junior Designer), James Stephenson (Designer), Jesper C. Nielsen (Design Manager), Adam Siegmund Grabowski (Senior Designer), Adam Corbally (Design Master), Justin Ramsden (Designer), Tobey-Louise Brown (Designer), Junya Suzuki (Senior Designer), John Cuppage (Senior Designer), Alice Geiger (Designer)

Due to the number of models for THE LEGO BATMAN MOVIE, a new team was created to work on the theme

How closely do you work with DC Comics?

Justin Ramsden: We work very closely with DC Comics to create the best toys possible. For instance, when designing sets for an upcoming film, we usually get to read the script way in advance of the movie being launched and decide on the moments (and characters) in the film that would translate best into LEGO sets. We also get sent a vast amount of reference images that we can base our models on. Some designers are even lucky enough to visit the movie set!

Esa Petteri Nousiainen working on the design for Batman's new bat-gear

How do you come up with ideas for new models?

Justin Ramsden: Design at the LEGO Group is a collaborative process. As LEGO model designers, we sit together with a creative lead and graphic designers to decide on fun new comic stories that we could look into, or DC Comics may send us reference for the latest movie or television series. We then create models based on these discussions and put them in the hands of children to see their reaction! After product tests, we go back and refine our designs until we come up with something we're proud of.

Bjarke Lykke Madsen looking at the Nightcrawler with Junya Suzuki and Alice Geiger

Mark Tranter with Tobey-Louise Brown and Adam Corbally looking at sketches of the Justice League Cyborg minifigure

What is the process for creating a new minifigure?

Adam Corbally: When creating a design for a minifigure that is based on a movie, we look at concept art and photos of the actors if we have them for reference. For non-movie products we look at all sorts of reference from comic books, TV shows, and cartoons. In both cases, we talk with DC about what we think works best. When we have a finished design, we send it to the LEGO factories to be printed and packed into the LEGO boxes.

121

Christopher Terrance Perron: The App-Controlled Batmobile was the hardest one so far. It was tricky trying to fit in all the necessary electronic components while still making a more streamlined model that would be stable when being driven around.

Christopher Terrance Peron and Brian Bering Larsen looking at designs for the App-Controlled Batmobile

Cyborg minifigure

Tobey-Louise Brown: The Speed Force Freeze Pursuit set (76098). Cyborg was the first detailed Super Heroes minifigure I worked on. It was a fun challenge fitting a character like this with a lot of detail into the minifigure form. Finding the right level of detail took a while. I made a few different variations and the design was finalized by Casper Glahder. The stickers for this set were also a good challenge, particularly the stickers for the helicopter tail. We added some red stickers to match bricks in the model. We put a lot of work into placing the stickers in the right place on the model.

Stickers on the helicopter tail

CYBORGCOPTER

Justin Ramsden: I really enjoyed designing the Lex Luthor mech in one of the most recent sets that I've worked on. LEGO Super Heroes have done a few mech suits before and it was a great task to try to add new functions into a completely new design of this iconic vehicle from the DC Comics universe.

Adam Siegmund Grabowski and Justin Ramsden looking at the Lex Luthor mech model

LEX LUTHOR MECH

Adjustable wings

BATWING

Bjarke Lykke Madsen: The Batwing from THE LEGO® BATMAN MOVIE, or the Knightcrawler from the *Justice League* movie. Both were very challenging because of complicated functions that must be designed in such a way that kids can build them.

> *"We make toys that inspire kids to construct, dream, and play in a fantastic universe."*
>
> JESPER C. NIELSEN

Which is your favorite vehicle and why?

Adam Grabowski: The 1966 Batmobile from the Classic Batcave set. By far. One of the reasons is that I am a huge fan of the guy who built the real car, George Barris (he is also responsible for a bunch of other TV vehicles). Some years ago, my boss at that time, Mauricio Bedolla, managed to take the prototype I made to Los Angeles and get it signed for me by George. That model is now proudly displayed in a glass cabinet at my home.

Red bat-symbol on car door

1960S BATMOBILE

John Cuppage: The Tumbler—it's an awesome model of an awesome Batman vehicle!

Christopher Terrance Perron: I really like The Tumbler, because it's such an awesome massive model and the source material from the Dark Knight Trilogy is really cool!

Suspension is made up of LEGO® Technic pieces

THE TUMBLER

Is there a minifigure that you'd love to see in the future?

Jesper C. Nielsen: I'd like to see more variants of Batwoman, Batgirl and the great female villians like Catwoman and Poison Ivy.

Justin Ramsden:
I'd love to see us look into creating more characters from the Bat-Family. Similarly, a Jessica Cruz minifigure would be awesome!

Alice Geiger: In general, I would love to see more superpower effects, like the head of Firestorm.

Firestorm and Cyborg minifigures with test molds for superpower elements

Which was the most challenging minifigure you have ever worked on?

Adam Corbally: Definitely the 2017 movie version of Cyborg. There were so many details in the reference to squeeze into such a tiny minifigure.

Sketch of the 2017 Cyborg minifigure from the set Flying Fox: Batmobile Airlift Attack (76087), which is based on the *Justice League* movie

"We have a lot of dialogue with DC to make the minifigure look as close to what we want."

CASPER GLAHDER

BATWOMAN

LOBO

LOBO'S SPACEHOG

Which is your favorite minifigure from the theme and why?

Casper Glahder: That would be the new Lobo minifigure I made. He is such a cool character and I am really happy we made him as a minifigure.

Justin Ramsden: I think that the Wonder Woman from the latest Justice League movie sets is amazing. It's brilliant to see how our LEGO graphic designers can shrink such a fantastic costume down into the iconic LEGO minifigure scale without losing any of the important details.

WONDER WOMAN

Sketch models of Lobo's Spacehog vehicle

SUPERMAN

If you could be any DC character for a day, who would you be?

Tobey-Louise Brown: If I could be a DC character, it would be Beast Boy so I could be an elephant for a day!

Bjarke Lykke Madsen: Superman, because he can do everything including flying and everybody dreams about flying, right?

BEAST BOY

INDEX

Page numbers in **bold** refer
to main entries

Penguin Random House

Senior Editor Victoria Taylor
Senior Designer Anna Formanek
Designer Gema Salamanca
Editorial Assistant Hannah Gulliver-Jones
Proofreader Jennette ElNaggar
Senior Pre-Production Producer Jennifer Murray
Senior Producer Lloyd Robertson
Managing Editor Paula Regan
Managing Art Editor Jo Connor
Art Director Lisa Lanzarini
Publisher Julie Ferris
Publishing Director Simon Beecroft

DK would like to thank: Randi Sørensen, Heidi K. Jensen, Martin Leighton Lindhardt. Paul Hansford, Justin Ramsden, Christopher Terrance Perron, Adam Siegmund Grabowski, Adam Corbally, Alice Geiger, Bjarke Lykke Madsen, Casper Glahder, Jesper C. Nielsen, John Cuppage, Junya Suzuki, Mark Tranter, Alice Kate Millard, James Stephenson, Michael Thomas Fuller, an Tobey-Louise Brown and Nikolaj Kristensen at the LEGO Group; Benjamin Harper, Thomas Zellers, and Jeff Neinstein at Warner Bros; and Alastair Dougall for editorial assistance.

First American Edition, 2018
Published in the United States by DK Publishing
345 Hudson Street, New York, New York 10014

Page design copyright © 2018 Dorling Kindersley Limited
DK, a Division of Penguin Random House LLC
18 19 20 21 22 10 9 8 7 6 5 4 3 2 1
001–308542–Sept/18

Published in Great Britain by
Dorling Kindersley Limited.

A catalog record for this book is available from the Library of Congress.

ISBN 978-1-4654-7545-9
ISBN 978-1-4654-7841-2 (library edition)

DK books are available at special discounts when purchased in bulk for sales promotions, premiums, fund-raising, or educational use. For details, contact: DK Publishing Special Markets, 345 Hudson Street, New York, New York 10014
SpecialSales@dk.com

Printed and bound in China

A WORLD OF IDEAS:
SEE ALL THERE IS TO KNOW

www.dk.com
www.LEGO.com